STRANGER MUSIC

BY LEONARD COHEN

BOOKS

Let Us Compare Mythologies   *1956*

The Spice-Box of Earth   *1961*

The Favourite Game   *1963*

Flowers for Hitler   *1964*

Beautiful Losers   *1966*

Parasites of Heaven   *1966*

Selected Poems, 1956–1968   *1968*

The Energy of Slaves   *1972*

Death of a Lady's Man   *1978*

Book of Mercy   *1984*

Stranger Music   *1993*

RECORDS

Songs of Leonard Cohen   *1967*

Songs from a Room   *1969*

Songs of Love and Hate   *1971*

Live Songs   *1972*

New Skin for the Old Ceremony   *1973*

The Best of Leonard Cohen   *1975*

Death of a Ladies' Man   *1977*

Recent Songs   *1979*

Various Positions   *1984*

I'm Your Man   *1988*

The Future   *1992*

STRANGER MUSIC

Selected Poems and Songs

LEONARD COHEN

JONATHAN CAPE
LONDON

First published in the United Kingdom in 1993

3   5   7   9   10   8   6   4

© Leonard Cohen and Leonard Cohen Stranger Music, Inc., 1993

First published in the United Kingdom in 1993 by Jonathan Cape
Random House, 20 Vauxhall Bridge Road, London SW1V 35A

Random House Australia (Pty) Limited
20 Alfred Street, Milsons Point, Sydney,
New South Wales, 2061, Australia

Random House New Zealand Limited
15 Poland Road, Glenfield,
Auckland 10, New Zealand

Random House South Africa (Pty) Limited
P.O. Box 337, Bergvlei, South Africa

Random House UK Limited Reg. No. 954009

A CIP catalogue record for this book
is available from the British Library

ISBN 0–224–03860–5

Printed in Great Britain by Clays Ltd., St. Ives PLC

A NOTE ON THE TEXT

In some sections of this book, certain poem titles and texts have been altered from their original publication.

In the section taken from *Death of a Lady's Man*, some changes have been made for this edition: "A Woman's Decision" originally appeared as the commentary to "The Lover After All"; "A Different Drum" as the commentary to "The Other Village"; "A Marvellous Woman" as the commentary to "No One Watching"; the text of "Not Going Back" is from the commentary to "The Rose"; the text of "Montreal" is from the commentary to "St. Francis"; "French and English" from the commentary to "Our Government-in-Exile"; "Roshi" originally appeared as the commentary to "Formal in His Thought of Her"; "The End of My Life in Art" originally appeared under the title "My Life in Art"; "Roshi Again" originally appeared as the commentary to "My Life in Art." The poems mentioned above have been given new titles for this edition. The poems in italic have, for this edition, incorporated the word "commentary" into the title.

Poems reproduced here from *Selected Poems 1956–1968* had original publication in that edition.

Selections from *Beautiful Losers* and *Book of Mercy* were given titles for this edition. All but three of the poems selected for this edition from *The Energy of Slaves* were originally untitled.

*   *   *

Nancy Bacal made the selection with the assistance of Rebecca De Mornay and the author. Bill Furey came up with a selection several years ago which was consulted. Karen Lynch and Kelley Lynch prepared the manuscript. Ellen Seligman, my editor at M&S, saw it through to publication. I want to thank all those concerned.

CONTENTS

SONGS OF LOVE AND HATE

THE ENERGY OF SLAVES

LET US COMPARE MYTHOLOGIES

POEM

I heard of a man
who says words so beautifully
that if he only speaks their name
women give themselves to him.

If I am dumb beside your body
while silence blossoms like tumours on our lips
it is because I hear a man climb the stairs
and clear his throat outside our door.

LETTER

How you murdered your family
means nothing to me
as your mouth moves across my body

And I know your dreams
of crumbling cities and galloping horses
of the sun coming too close
and the night never ending

but these mean nothing to me
beside your body

I know that outside a war is raging
that you issue orders
that babies are smothered and generals beheaded

but blood means nothing to me
it does not disturb your flesh

tasting blood on your tongue
does not shock me
as my arms grow into your hair

Do not think I do not understand
what happens
after the troops have been massacred
and the harlots put to the sword

And I write this only to rob you

that when one morning my head
hangs dripping with the other generals
from your house gate

that all this was anticipated
and so you will know that it meant nothing to me

LOVERS

During the first pogrom they
Met behind the ruins of their homes —
Sweet merchants trading: her love
For a history-full of poems.

And at the hot ovens they
Cunningly managed a brief
Kiss before the soldier came
To knock out her golden teeth.

And in the furnace itself
As the flames flamed higher,
He tried to kiss her burning breasts
As she burned in the fire.

Later he often wondered:
Was their barter completed?
While men around him plundered
And knew he had been cheated.

PRAYER FOR MESSIAH

His blood on my arm is warm as a bird
his heart in my hand is heavy as lead
his eyes through my eyes shine brighter than love
O send out the raven ahead of the dove

His life in my mouth is less than a man
his death on my breast is harder than stone
his eyes through my eyes shine brighter than love
O send out the raven ahead of the dove

O send out the raven ahead of the dove
O sing from your chains where you're chained in a cave
your eyes through my eyes shine brighter than love
your blood in my ballad collapses the grave

O sing from your chains where you're chained in a cave
your eyes through my eyes shine brighter than love
your heart in my hand is heavy as lead
your blood on my arm is warm as a bird

O break from your branches a green branch of love
after the raven has died for the dove

WHEN THIS AMERICAN WOMAN

When this American woman,
whose thighs are bound in casual red cloth,
comes thundering past my sitting-place
like a forest-burning Mongol tribe,
the city is ravished
and brittle buildings of a hundred years
splash into the street;
and my eyes are burnt
for the embroidered Chinese girls,
already old,
and so small between the thin pines
on these enormous landscapes,
that if you turn your head
they are lost for hours.

THESE HEROICS

If I had a shining head
and people turned to stare at me
in the streetcars;
and I could stretch my body
through the bright water
and keep abreast of fish and water snakes;
if I could ruin my feathers
in flight before the sun;
do you think that I would remain in this room,
reciting poems to you,
and making outrageous dreams
with the smallest movements of your mouth?

WARNING

If your neighbour disappears
O if your neighbour disappears
The quiet man who raked his lawn
The girl who always took the sun

Never mention it to your wife
Never say at dinner time
Whatever happened to that man
Who used to rake his lawn

Never say to your daughter
As you're walking home from church
Funny thing about that girl
I haven't seen her for a month

And if your son says to you
Nobody lives next door
They've all gone away
Send him to bed with no supper

Because it can spread, it can spread
And one fine evening coming home
Your wife and daughter and son
They'll have caught the idea and will be gone

THE FLY

In his black armour
    the house-fly marched the field
of Freda's sleeping thighs,
undisturbed by the soft hand
    which vaguely moved
to end his exercise.

And it ruined my day —
    this fly which never planned
to charm her or to please
should walk boldly on that ground
    I tried so hard
to lay my trembling knees.

THE SPICE-BOX OF EARTH

AS THE MIST LEAVES NO SCAR

As the mist leaves no scar
On the dark green hill,
So my body leaves no scar
On you, nor ever will.

When wind and hawk encounter,
What remains to keep?
So you and I encounter,
Then turn, then fall to sleep.

As many nights endure
Without a moon or star,
So will we endure
When one is gone and far.

BENEATH MY HANDS

Beneath my hands
your small breasts
are the upturned bellies
of breathing fallen sparrows.

Wherever you move
I hear the sounds of closing wings
of falling wings.

I am speechless
because you have fallen beside me
because your eyelashes
are the spines of tiny fragile animals.

I dread the time
when your mouth
begins to call me hunter.

When you call me close
to tell me
your body is not beautiful
I want to summon
the eyes and hidden mouths
of stone and light and water
to testify against you.

I want them
to surrender before you
the trembling rhyme of your face
from their deep caskets.

When you call me close
to tell me
your body is not beautiful
I want my body and my hands
to be pools
for your looking and laughing.

I HAVE NOT LINGERED IN
EUROPEAN MONASTERIES

I have not lingered in European monasteries
and discovered among the tall grasses tombs of knights
who fell as beautifully as their ballads tell;
I have not parted the grasses
or purposefully left them thatched.

I have not released my mind to wander and wait
in those great distances
between the snowy mountains and the fishermen,
like a moon,
or a shell beneath the moving water.

I have not held my breath
so that I might hear the breathing of G-d,
or tamed my heartbeat with an exercise,
or starved for visions.
Although I have watched him often
I have not become the heron,
leaving my body on the shore,
and I have not become the luminous trout,
leaving my body in the air.

I have not worshipped wounds and relics,
or combs of iron,
or bodies wrapped and burnt in scrolls.

I have not been unhappy for ten thousand years.
During the day I laugh and during the night I sleep.
My favourite cooks prepare my meals,
my body cleans and repairs itself,
and all my work goes well.

I LONG TO HOLD SOME LADY

I long to hold some lady
For my love is far away,
And will not come tomorrow
And was not here today.

There is no flesh so perfect
As on my lady's bone,
And yet it seems so distant
When I am all alone:

As though she were a masterpiece
In some castled town,
That pilgrims come to visit
And priests to copy down.

Alas, I cannot travel
To a love I have so deep
Or sleep too close beside
A love I want to keep.

But I long to hold some lady,
For flesh is warm and sweet.
Cold skeletons go marching
Each night beside my feet.

OWNING EVERYTHING

You worry that I will leave you.
I will not leave you.
Only strangers travel.
Owning everything,
I have nowhere to go.

SONG

I almost went to bed
without remembering
the four white violets
I put in the button-hole
of your green sweater

and how I kissed you then
and you kissed me
shy as though I'd
never been your lover

FOR ANNE

With Annie gone,
Whose eyes to compare
With the morning sun?

Not that I did compare,
But I do compare
Now that she's gone.

YOU HAVE THE LOVERS

You have the lovers,
they are nameless, their histories only for each other,
and you have the room, the bed and the windows.
Pretend it is a ritual.
Unfurl the bed, bury the lovers, blacken the windows,
let them live in that house for a generation or two.
No one dares disturb them.
Visitors in the corridor tiptoe past the long closed door,
they listen for sounds, for a moan, for a song:
nothing is heard, not even breathing.
You know they are not dead,
you can feel the presence of their intense love.
Your children grow up, they leave you,
they have become soldiers and riders.
Your mate dies after a life of service.
Who knows you? Who remembers you?
But in your house a ritual is in progress:
it is not finished: it needs more people.
One day the door is opened to the lover's chambers.
The room has become a dense garden,
full of colours, smells, sounds you have never known.
The bed is smooth as a wafer of sunlight,
in the midst of the garden it stands alone.
In the bed the lovers, slowly and deliberately and silently,
perform the act of love.
Their eyes are closed,
as tightly as if heavy coins of flesh lay on them.
Their lips are bruised with new and old bruises.
Her hair and his beard are hopelessly tangled.
When he puts his mouth against her shoulder
she is uncertain whether her shoulder

has given or received the kiss.
All her flesh is like a mouth.
He carries his fingers along her waist
and feels his own waist caressed.
She holds him closer and his own arms tighten around her.
She kisses the hand beside her mouth.
It is his hand or her hand, it hardly matters,
there are so many more kisses.
You stand beside the bed, weeping with happiness,
you carefully peel away the sheets
from the slow-moving bodies.
Your eyes are filled with tears, you barely make out the lovers.
As you undress you sing out, and your voice is magnificent
because now you believe it is the first human voice
heard in that room.
The garments you let fall grow into vines.
You climb into bed and recover the flesh.
You close your eyes and allow them to be sewn shut.
You create an embrace and fall into it.
There is only one moment of pain or doubt
as you wonder how many multitudes are lying beside your body,
but a mouth kisses and a hand soothes the moment away.

SONG FOR ABRAHAM KLEIN

The weary psalmist paused
His instrument beside.
Departed was the Sabbath
And the Sabbath Bride.

The table was decayed,
The candles black and cold.
The bread he sang so beautifully,
That bread was mould.

He turned toward his lute,
Trembling in the night.
He thought he knew no music
To make the morning right.

Abandoned was the Law,
Abandoned the King.
Unaware he took his instrument,
His habit was to sing.

He sang and nothing changed
Though many heard the song.
But soon his face was beautiful
And soon his limbs were strong.

SONG TO MAKE ME STILL

Lower your eyelids
over the water
Join the night
like the trees
you lie under

How many crickets
how many waves
easy after easy
on the one-way shore

There are stars
from another view
and a moon
to draw the seaweed through

No one calls the crickets vain
in their time
in their time
No one will call you idle
for dying with the sun

SUMMER HAIKU
for Frank and Marian Scott

Silence
and a deeper silence
when the crickets
hesitate

MY LADY CAN SLEEP

My lady can sleep
Upon a handkerchief
Or if it be Fall
Upon a fallen leaf.

I have seen the hunters
Kneel before her hem —
Even in her sleep
She turns away from them.

The only gift they offer
Is their abiding grief —
I pull out my pockets
For a handkerchief or leaf.

GIFT

You tell me that silence
is nearer to peace than poems
but if for my gift
I brought you silence
(for I know silence)
you would say
This is not silence
this is another poem
and you would hand it back to me.

I WONDER HOW MANY PEOPLE
IN THIS CITY

I wonder how many people in this city
live in furnished rooms.
Late at night when I look out at the buildings
I swear I see a face in every window
looking back at me,
and when I turn away
I wonder how many go back to their desks
and write this down.

TRAVEL

Loving you, flesh to flesh, I often thought
Of travelling penniless to some mud throne
Where a master might instruct me how to plot
My life away from pain, to love alone
In the bruiseless embrace of stone and lake.

Lost in the fields of your hair I was never lost
Enough to lose a way I had to take;
Breathless beside your body I could not exhaust
The will that forbid me contract, vow,
Or promise, and often while you slept
I looked in awe beyond your beauty.

                   Now
I know why many men have stopped and wept
Halfway between the loves they leave and seek,
And wondered if travel leads them anywhere —
Horizons keep the soft line of your cheek,
The windy sky's a locket for your hair.

I HAVE TWO BARS OF SOAP

I have two bars of soap,
the fragrance of almond,
one for you and one for me.
Draw the bath,
we will wash each other.

I have no money,
I murdered the pharmacist.

And here's a jar of oil,
just like in the Bible.
Lie in my arms,
I'll make your flesh glisten.

I have no money,
I murdered the perfumer.

Look through the window
at the shops and people.
Tell me what you desire,
you'll have it by the hour.

I have no money,
I have no money.

THE CUCKOLD'S SONG

If this looks like a poem
I might as well warn you at the beginning
that it's not meant to be one.
I don't want to turn anything into poetry.
I know all about her part in it
but I'm not concerned with that right now.
This is between you and me.
Personally I don't give a damn who led who on:
in fact I wonder if I give a damn at all.
But a man's got to say something.
Anyhow you fed her 5 MacKewan Ales,
took her to your room, put the right records on,
and in an hour or two it was done.
I know all about passion and honour
but unfortunately this had really nothing to do with either:
oh there was passion I'm only too sure
and even a little honour
but the important thing was to cuckold Leonard Cohen.
Hell, I might just as well address this to the both of you:
I haven't time to write anything else.
I've got to say my prayers.
I've got to wait by the window.
I repeat: the important thing was to cuckold Leonard Cohen.
I like that line because it's got my name in it.
What really makes me sick
is that everything goes on as it went before:
I'm still a sort of friend,
I'm still a sort of lover.
But not for long:

that's why I'm telling this to the two of you.
The fact is I'm turning to gold, turning to gold.
It's a long process, they say,
it happens in stages.
This is to inform you that I've already turned to clay.

MORNING SONG

She dreamed the doctors arrived
And severed her legs at the knee.
This she dreamed on a morning
Of a night she slept beside me.

Now I was not in this dream
Or the cry of the amputee,
Yet she told me this on a morning
Of a night she slept beside me.

THE FLOWERS THAT I LEFT
IN THE GROUND

The flowers that I left in the ground,
that I did not gather for you,
today I bring them all back,
to let them grow forever,
not in poems or marble,
but where they fell and rotted.

And the ships in their great stalls,
huge and transitory as heroes,
ships I could not captain,
today I bring them back
to let them sail forever,
not in model or ballad,
but where they were wrecked and scuttled.

And the child on whose shoulders I stand,
whose longing I purged
with public, kingly discipline,
today I bring him back
to languish forever,
not in confession or biography,
but where he flourished,
growing sly and hairy.

It is not malice that draws me away,
draws me to renunciation, betrayal:
it is weariness, I go for weariness of thee.
Gold, ivory, flesh, love, G-d, blood, moon —
I have become the expert of the catalogue.

My body once so familiar with glory,
my body has become a museum:
this part remembered because of someone's mouth,
this because of a hand,
this of wetness, this of heat.

Who owns anything he has not made?
With your beauty I am as uninvolved
as with horses' manes and waterfalls.
This is my last catalogue.
I breathe the breathless
I love you, I love you —
and let you move forever.

A KITE IS A VICTIM

A kite is a victim you are sure of.
You love it because it pulls
gentle enough to call you master,
strong enough to call you fool;
because it lives
like a trained falcon
in the high sweet air,
and you can always haul it down
to tame it in your drawer.

A kite is a fish you have already caught
in a pool where no fish come,
so you play him carefully and long,
and hope he won't give up,
or the wind die down.

A kite is the last poem you've written,
so you give it to the wind,
but you don't let it go
until someone finds you
something else to do.

A kite is a contract of glory
that must be made with the sun,
so you make friends with the field
the river and the wind,
then you pray the whole cold night before,
under the travelling cordless moon,
to make you worthy and lyric and pure.

THERE ARE SOME MEN

There are some men
who should have mountains
to bear their names to time.

Grave-markers are not high enough
or green,
and sons go far away
to lose the fist
their father's hand will always seem.

I had a friend:
he lived and died in mighty silence
and with dignity,
left no book, son, or lover to mourn.

Nor is this a mourning-song
but only a naming of this mountain
on which I walk,
fragrant, dark, and softly white
under the pale of mist.
I name this mountain after him.

ISAIAH
for G.C.S.

Between the mountains of spices
the cities thrust up pearl domes and filigree spires.
Never before was Jerusalem so beautiful.
     In the sculptured temple how many pilgrims,
lost in the measures of tambourine and lyre,
kneeled before the glory of the ritual?
     Trained in grace the daughters of Zion moved,
not less splendid than the golden statuary,
the bravery of ornaments about their scented feet.
     Government was done in palaces.
Judges, their fortunes found in law,
reclining and cosmopolitan, praised reason.
Commerce like a strong wild garden
     flourished in the street.
The coins were bright, the crest on coins precise,
new ones looked almost wet.

Why did Isaiah rage and cry,
Jersusalem is ruined,
     your cities are burned with fire?

On the fragrant hills of Gilboa
were the shepherds ever calmer,
the sheep fatter, the white wool whiter?
     There were fig trees, cedar, orchards
where men worked in perfume all day long.
New mines as fresh as pomegranates.
     Robbers were gone from the roads,
     the highways were straight.
There were years of wheat against famine.

Enemies? Who has heard of a righteous state
    that has no enemies,
but the young were strong, archers cunning,
    their arrows accurate.

Why then this fool Isaiah,
smelling vaguely of wilderness himself,
why did he shout,
    Your country is desolate?

Now will I sing to my well-beloved
a song of my beloved touching her hair
which is pure metal black
    no rebel prince can change to dross,
of my beloved touching her body
    no false swearer can corrupt,
of my beloved touching her mind
    no faithless counsellor can inflame,
of my beloved touching the mountains of spices
making them beauty instead of burning.

Now plunged in unutterable love
Isaiah wanders, chosen, stumbling
against the sculptured walls which consume
their full age in his embrace and powder
as he goes by. He reels beyond
    the falling dust of spires and domes,
obliterating ritual: the Holy Name, half-spoken,
is lost on the cantor's tongue; their pages barren,
congregations blink, agonized and dumb.
    In the turns of his journey
heavy trees he sleeps under
mature into cinder and crumble:
    whole orchards join the wind
like rising flocks of ravens.

The rocks go back to water, the water to waste.
And while Isaiah gently hums a sound
to make the guilty country uncondemned,
     all men, truthfully desolate and lonely,
as though witnessing a miracle,
behold in beauty the faces of one another.

FLOWERS FOR HITLER

WHAT I'M DOING HERE

I do not know if the world has lied
I have lied
I do not know if the world has conspired against love
I have conspired against love
The atmosphere of torture is no comfort
I have tortured
Even without the mushroom cloud
still I would have hated
Listen
I would have done the same things
even if there were no death
I will not be held like a drunkard
under the cold tap of facts
I refuse the universal alibi

Like an empty telephone booth passed at night
and remembered
like mirrors in a movie palace lobby consulted
only on the way out
like a nymphomaniac who binds a thousand
into strange brotherhood
I wait
for each one of you to confess

I WANTED TO BE A DOCTOR

The famous doctor held up Grandma's stomach.
Cancer! Cancer! he cried out.
The theatre was brought low.
None of the interns thought about ambition.

Cancer! They all looked the other way.
They thought Cancer would leap out
and get them. They hated to be near.
This happened in Vilna in the Medical School.

Nobody could sit still.
They might be sitting beside Cancer.
Cancer was present.
Cancer had been let out of its bottle.

I was looking in the skylight.
I wanted to be a doctor.
All the interns ran outside.
The famous doctor held on to the stomach.

He was alone with Cancer.
Cancer! Cancer! Cancer!
He didn't care who heard or didn't hear.
It was his 87th Cancer.

THE DRAWER'S CONDITION
ON NOVEMBER 28, 1961

Is there anything emptier
than the drawer where
you used to store your opium?
How like a black-eyed Susan
blinded into ordinary daisy
is my pretty kitchen drawer!
How like a nose sans nostrils
is my bare wooden drawer!
How like an eggless basket!
How like a pool sans tortoise!
My hand has explored
my drawer like a rat
in an experiment of mazes.
Reader, I may safely say
there's not an emptier drawer
in all of Christendom!

THE INVISIBLE TROUBLE

Too fevered to insist:
"My world is terror,"
he covers his wrist
and numbers of the war.

His arm is unburned
his flesh whole:
the numbers he learned
from a movie reel.

He covers his wrist
under the table.
The drunkards have missed
his invisible trouble.

A tune rises up.
His skin is blank!
He can't lift his cup
he can't! he can't!

The chorus grows.
So does his silence.
Nothing, he knows
there is nothing to notice.

OPIUM AND HITLER

Several faiths
bid him leap —
opium and Hitler
let him sleep.

A Negress with
an appetite
helped him think
he wasn't white.

Opium and Hitler
made him sure
the world was glass.
There was no cure

for matter
disarmed as this:
the state rose on
a festered kiss.

Once a dream
nailed on the sky
a summer sun
while it was high.

He wanted a
blindfold of skin,
he wanted the
afternoon to begin.

One law broken —
nothing held.
The world was wax,
his to mould.

No! He fumbled
for his history dose.
The sun came loose,
his woman close.

Lost in a darkness
their bodies would reach,
the Leader started
a racial speech.

IT USES US!

Come upon this heap
exposed to camera leer:
would you snatch a skull
for midnight wine, my dear?

Can you wear a cape,
claim these burned for you
or is this death unusable
alien and new?

In our leaders' faces
(albeit they deplore
the past) can you read how
they love Freedom more?

In my own mirror
their eyes beam at me:
my face is theirs, my eyes
burnt and free.

Now you and I are mounted
on this heap, my dear:
from this height we thrill
as boundaries disappear.

Kiss me with your teeth
All things can be done
whisper museum ovens of
a war that Freedom won.

HEIRLOOM

The torture scene developed under a glass bell
such as might protect an expensive clock.
I almost expected a chime to sound
as the tongs were applied
and the body jerked and fainted calm.
All the people were tiny and rosy-cheeked
and if I could have heard a cry of triumph or pain
it would have been tiny as the mouth that made it
or one single note of a music box.
The drama bell was mounted
like a gigantic baroque pearl
on a wedding ring or brooch or locket.
    I know you feel naked, little darling.
I know you hate living in the country
and can't wait until the shiny magazines
come every week and every month.
Look through your grandmother's house again.
There is an heirloom somewhere.

ALL THERE IS TO KNOW ABOUT
ADOLPH EICHMANN

EYES: . . . . Medium
HAIR: . . . . Medium
WEIGHT: . . . . Medium
HEIGHT: . . . . Medium
DISTINGUISHING FEATURES: . . . . None
NUMBER OF FINGERS: . . . . Ten
NUMBER OF TOES: . . . . Ten
INTELLIGENCE: . . . . Medium

What did you expect?
Talons?
Oversize incisors?
Green saliva?

Madness?

SKY

The great ones pass
they pass without touching
they pass without looking
each in his joy
each in his fire
Of one another
they have no need
they have the deepest need
The great ones pass

Recorded in some multiple sky
inlaid in some endless laughter
they pass
like stars of different seasons
like meteors of different centuries

Fire undiminished
by passing fire
laughter uncorroded
by comfort
they pass one another
without touching without looking
needing only to know
the great ones pass

HITLER

Now let him go to sleep with history,
the real skeleton stinking of gasoline,
the Mutt-and-Jeff henchmen beside him:
let them sleep among our precious poppies.

Cadres of SS waken in our minds
where they began before we ransomed them
to that actual empty realm we people
with the shadows that disturb our inward peace.

For a while we resist the silver-black cars
rolling in slow parade through the brain.
We stuff the microphones with old chaotic flowers
from a bed which rapidly exhausts itself.

Never mind. They turn up as poppies
beside the tombs and libraries of the real world.
The leader's vast design, the tilt of his chin
seem excessively familiar to minds at peace.

THE FAILURE OF A SECULAR LIFE

The pain-monger came home
from a hard day's torture.

He came home with his tongs.
He put down his black bag.

His wife hit him with an open nerve
and a cry the trade never heard.

He watched her real-life Dachau,
knew his career was ruined.

Was there anything else to do?
He sold his bag and tongs,

went to pieces. A man's got to be able
to bring his wife something.

WHEELS, FIRECLOUDS

I shot my eyes through the drawers of your empty coffins,
I was loyal,
I was one who lifted up his face.

THE MUSIC CREPT BY US

I would like to remind
the management
that the drinks are watered
and the hat-check girl
has syphilis
and the band is composed
of former SS monsters
However since it is
New Year's Eve
and I have lip cancer
I will place my
paper hat on my
concussion and dance

HYDRA 1960

Anything that moves is white,
a gull, a wave, a sail,
and moves too purely to be aped.
Smash the pain.

Never pretend peace.
The consolumentum has not,
never will be kissed. Pain
cannot compromise this light.

Do violence to the pain,
ruin the easy vision,
the easy warning, water
for those who need to burn.

These are ruthless: rooster shriek,
bleached goat skull.
Scalpels grow with poppies
if you see them truly red.

QUEEN VICTORIA AND ME

Queen Victoria
my father and all his tobacco loved you
I love you too in all your forms
the slim unlovely virgin anyone would lay
the white figure floating among German beards
the mean governess of the huge pink maps
the solitary mourner of a prince
Queen Victoria
I am cold and rainy
I am dirty as a glass roof in a train station
I feel like an empty cast-iron exhibition
I want ornaments on everything
because my love she gone with other boys
Queen Victoria
do you have a punishment under the white lace
will you be short with her
and make her read little Bibles
will you spank her with a mechanical corset
I want her pure as power
I want her skin slightly musty with petticoats
will you wash the easy bidets out of her head
Queen Victoria
I'm not much nourished by modern love
Will you come into my life
with your sorrow and your black carriages
and your perfect memory
Queen Victory
The 20th century belongs to you and me
Let us be two severe giants
(not less lonely for our partnership)

who discolour test tubes in the halls of science
who turn up unwelcome at every World's Fair
heavy with proverb and correction
confusing the star-dazed tourists
with our incomparable sense of loss

I HAD IT FOR A MOMENT

I had it for a moment
I knew why I must thank you
    I saw powerful governing men in black suits
I saw them undressed
in the arms of young mistresses
the men more naked than the naked women
the men crying quietly
    No that is not it
I'm losing why I must thank you
which means I'm left with pure longing
    How old are you
Do you like your thighs
I had it for a moment
I had a reason for letting the picture
of your mouth destroy my conversation
    Something on the radio
the end of a Mexican song
I saw the musicians getting paid
they are not even surprised
they knew it was only a job
    Now I've lost it completely
A lot of people think you are beautiful
How do I feel about that
I have no feeling about that
    I had a wonderful reason for not merely
courting you
It was tied up with the newspapers
    I saw secret arrangements in high offices
I saw men who loved their worldliness
even though they had looked through
big electric telescopes

they still thought their worldliness was serious
not just a hobby a taste a harmless affectation
    they thought the cosmos listened
I was suddenly fearful
one of their obscure regulations
could separate us
    I was ready to beg for mercy
Now I'm getting into humiliation
I've lost why I began this
I wanted to talk about your eyes
I know nothing about your eyes
and you've noticed how little I know
I want you somewhere safe
far from high offices
    I'll study you later
So many people want to cry quietly beside you

July 4, 1963

THE WAY BACK

But I am not lost
any more than leaves are lost
or buried vases
This is not my time
I would only give you second thoughts

I know you must call me traitor
because I have wasted my blood
in aimless love
and you are right
Blood like that
never won an inch of star

You know how to call me
although such a noise now
would only confuse the air
Neither of us can forget
the steps we danced
the words you stretched
to call me out of dust

Yes I long for you
not just as a leaf for weather
or vase for hands
but with a narrow human longing
that makes a man refuse
any fields but his own

I wait for you at an
unexpected place in your journey
like the rusted key
or the feather you do not pick up
until the way back
after it is clear
the remote and painful destination
changed nothing in your life

ON HEARING A NAME
LONG UNSPOKEN

Listen to the stories
men tell of last year
that sound of other places
though they happened here

Listen to a name
so private it can burn
hear it said aloud
and learn and learn

History is a needle
for putting men asleep
anointed with the poison
of all they want to keep

Now a name that saved you
has a foreign taste
claims a foreign body
froze in last year's waste

And what is living lingers
while monuments are built
then yields its final whisper
to letters raised in gilt

But cries of stifled ripeness
whip me to my knees
I am with the falling snow
falling in the seas

I am with the hunters
hungry and shrewd
and I am with the hunted
quick and soft and nude

I am with the houses
that wash away in rain
and leave no teeth of pillars
to rake them up again

Let men numb names
scratch winds that blow
listen to the stories
but what you know you know

And knowing is enough
for mountains such as these
where nothing long remains
houses walls or trees

STYLE

I don't believe the radio stations
of Russia and America
but I like the music and I like
the solemn European voices announcing jazz
I don't believe opium or money
though they're hard to get
and punished with long sentences
I don't believe love
in the midst of my slavery I
do not believe
I am man sitting in a house
on a treeless Argolic island
I will forget the grass of my mother's lawn
I know I will
I will forget the old telephone number
Fitzroy seven eight two oh
I will forget my style
I will have no style
I hear a thousand miles of hungry static
and the old clear water eating rocks
I hear the bells of mules eating
I hear the flowers eating the night
under their folds
Now a rooster with a razor
plants the haemophilia gash across
the soft black sky
and now I know for certain
I will forget my style
Perhaps a mind will open in this world
perhaps a heart will catch rain
Nothing will heal and nothing will freeze

but perhaps a heart will catch rain
America will have no style
Russia will have no style
It is happening in the twenty-eighth year
of my attention
I don't know what will become
of the mules with their lady eyes
or the old clear water
or the giant rooster
The early morning greedy radio eats
the governments one by one the languages
the poppy fields one by one
Beyond the numbered band
a silence develops for every style
for the style I laboured on
an external silence like the space
between insects in a swarm
electric unremembering
and it is aimed at us
(I am sleepy and frightened)
it is upon us brothers

DISGUISES

I am sorry that the rich man must go
and his house become a hospital.
I loved his wine, his contemptuous servants,
his ten-year-old ceremonies.
I loved his car which he wore like a snail's shell
everywhere, and I loved his wife,
the hours she put into her skin,
the milk, the lust, the industries
that served her complexion.
I loved his son who looked British
but had American ambitions
and let the word aristocrat comfort him
like a reprieve while Kennedy reigned.
I loved the rich man: I hate to see
his season ticket for the Opera
fall into a pool for opera-lovers.

I am sorry that the old worker must go
who called me mister when I was twelve
and sir when I was twenty
who studied against me in obscure socialist
clubs which met in restaurants.
I loved the machine he knew like a wife's body.
I loved his wife who trained bankers
in an underground pantry
and never wasted her ambition in ceramics.
I loved his children who debate
and come first at McGill University.
Goodbye old gold-watch winner
all your complex loyalties
must now be borne by one-faced patriots.

Goodbye dope fiends of North Eastern Lunch
circa 1948, your spoons which were not
Swedish Stainless, were the same colour
as the hoarded clasps and hooks
of discarded soiled therapeutic corsets.
I loved your puns about snow
even if they lasted the full seven-month
Montreal winter. Go write your memoirs
for the Psychedelic Review.

Goodbye sex fiends of Beaver Pond
who dreamed of being jacked-off
by electric milking machines.
You had no Canada Council.
You had to open little boys
with a pen-knife.
I loved your statement to the press:
"I didn't think he'd mind."
Goodbye articulate monsters
Abbott and Costello have met Frankenstein.

I am sorry that the conspirators must go
the ones who scared me by showing me
a list of all the members of my family.
I loved the way they reserved judgement
about Genghis Khan. They loved me because
I told them their little beards
made them dead-ringers for Lenin.
The bombs went off in Westmount
and now they are ashamed
like a successful outspoken Schopenhauerian
whose room-mate has committed suicide.
Suddenly they are all making movies.
I have no one to buy coffee for.

I embrace the changeless:
the committed men in public wards
oblivious as Hassidim
who believe that they are someone else.
Bravo! Abelard, viva! Rockefeller,
have these buns, Napoleon,
hurrah! betrayed Duchess.
Long live you chronic self-abusers!
you monotheists!
you familiars of the Absolute
sucking at circles!

You are all my comfort
as I turn to face the beehive
as I disgrace my style
as I coarsen my nature
as I invent jokes
as I pull up my garters
as I accept responsibility.

You comfort me
incorrigible betrayers of the self
as I salute fashion
and bring my mind
        like a promiscuous air-hostess
handing out parachutes in a nose dive
bring my butchered mind
to bear upon the facts.

CHERRY ORCHARDS

Canada some wars are waiting for you
some threats
some torn flags
Inheritance is not enough
    Faces must be forged under the hammer
of savage ideas
    Mailboxes will explode
in the cherry orchards
and somebody will wait forever
for his grandfather's fat cheque
    From my deep café I survey the quiet snowfields
like a U.S. promoter
of a new plastic snowshoe
looking for a moving speck
a troika perhaps
an exile
an icy prophet
an Indian insurrection
a burning weather station
    There's a story out there boys
Canada could you bear some folk songs
about freedom and death

STREETCARS

Did you see the streetcars
passing as of old
along Ste Catherine Street?
Golden streetcars
passing under the tearful
Temple of the Heart
where the crutches hang
like catatonic divining twigs.
A thin young priest
folds his semen in a kleenex
his face glowing
in the passing gold
as the world returns.
A lovely riot gathers the citizenry
into its spasms
as the past comes back
in the form of golden streetcars.
I carry a banner:
"The Past Is Perfect."
My little female cousin
who does not believe
in our religious destiny
rides royally on my nostalgia.
The streetcars curtsy
round a corner.
Firecrackers and moths
drip from their humble wires.

NOTHING I CAN LOSE

When I left my father's house
the sun was halfway up,
my father held it to my chin
like a buttercup.

My father was a snake-oil man
a wizard, trickster, liar,
but this was his best trick,
we kissed goodbye in fire.

A mile above Niagara Falls
a dove gave me the news
of his death. I didn't miss a step,
there's nothing I can lose.

Tomorrow I'll invent a trick
I do not know tonight,
the wind, the pole will tell me what
and the friendly blinding light.

FRONT LAWN

The snow was falling
over my penknife
There was a movie
in the fireplace
The apples were wrapped
in 8-year-old blonde hair
Starving and dirty
the janitor's daughter never
turned up in November
to pee from her sweet crack
on the gravel
    I'll go back one day
when my cast is off
Elm leaves are falling
over my bow and arrow
Candy is going bad
and Boy Scout calendars
are on fire
    My old mother
sits in her Cadillac
laughing her Danube laugh
as I tell her that we own
all the worms
under our front lawn
    Rust rust rust
in the engines of love and time

THE BIG WORLD

The big world will find out
about this farm
the big world will learn
the details of what
I worked out in the can

And your curious life with me
will be told so often
that no one will believe
you grew old

THE LISTS

Strafed by the Milky Way
vaccinated by a snarl of clouds
lobotomized by the bore of the moon
he fell in a heap
some woman's smell
smeared across his face
a plan for Social Welfare
rusting in a trouser cuff
    From five to seven
tall trees doctored him
mist roamed on guard
    Then it began again
the sun stuck a gun in his mouth
the wind started to skin him
Give up the Plan give up the Plan
echoing among its scissors
    The women who elected him
performed erotic calisthenics
above the stock-reports
of his and every hero's fame
    Out of the corner of his stuffed eye
etched in minor metal
under his letter of the alphabet
he clearly saw his tiny name
    Then a museum slid under
his remains like a shovel

PROMISE

Your blonde hair
is the way I live —
smashed by light!

Your mouth-print
is the birthmark
on my power.

To love you
is to live
my ideal diary

which I have
promised my body
I will never write!

FOR E.J.P.

I once believed a single line
    in a Chinese poem could change
        forever how blossoms fell
and that the moon itself climbed on
    the grief of concise weeping men
        to journey over cups of wine
I thought invasions were begun for crows
    to pick at a skeleton
        dynasties sown and spent
to serve the language of a fine lament
    I thought governors ended their lives
        as sweetly drunken monks
telling time by rain and candles
    instructed by an insect's pilgrimage
        across the page — all this
so one might send an exile's perfect letter
to an ancient hometown friend

I chose a lonely country
    broke from love
        scorned the fraternity of war
I polished my tongue against the pumice moon
    floated my soul in cherry wine
        a perfumed barge for Lords of Memory
to languish on to drink to whisper out
    their store of strength
        as if beyond the mist along the shore
their girls their power still obeyed
    like clocks wound for a thousand years
I waited until my tongue was sore

Brown petals wind like fire around my poems
    I aimed them at the stars but
       like rainbows they were bent
before they sawed the world in half
    Who can trace the canyoned paths
       cattle have carved out of time
wandering from meadowlands to feasts
    Layer after layer of autumn leaves
       are swept away
Something forgets us perfectly

PARASITES OF HEAVEN

ONE NIGHT I BURNED

One night I burned the house I loved,
It lit a perfect ring
In which I saw some weeds and stone
Beyond — not anything.

Certain creatures of the air
Frightened by the night,
They came to see the world again
And perished in the light.

Now I sail from sky to sky
And all the blackness sings
Against the boat that I have made
Of mutilated wings.

1960

I SEE YOU ON A GREEK MATTRESS

I see you on a Greek mattress
reading the *Book of Changes*,
Lebanese candy in the air.
On the whitewashed wall I see
you raise another hexagram
for the same old question:
how can you be free?
I see you cleaning your pipe
with the hairpin
of somebody's innocent night.
I see the plastic Evil Eye
pinned to your underwear.
Once again you throw the pennies,
once again you read
how the pieces of the world
have changed around your question.
Did you get to the Himalayas?
Did you visit that monk in New Jersey?
I never answered any of your letters.
Oh Steve, do you remember me?

1963

SNOW IS FALLING

Snow is falling.
There is a nude in my room.
She surveys the wine-coloured carpet.

She is eighteen.
She has straight hair.
She speaks no Montreal language.

She doesn't feel like sitting down.
She shows no gooseflesh.
We can hear the storm.

She is lighting a cigarette
from the gas range.
She holds back her long hair.

1958

FINGERPRINTS

Give me back my fingerprints
My fingertips are raw
If I don't get my fingerprints
I have to call the Law

I touched you once too often
& I don't know who I am
My fingerprints were missing
When I wiped away the jam

I called my fingerprints all night
But they don't seem to care
The last time that I saw them
They were leafing thru your hair

I thought I'd leave this morning
So I emptied out your drawer
A hundred thousand fingerprints
Floated to the floor

You hardly stooped to pick them up
You don't count what you lose
You don't even seem to know
Whose fingerprints are whose

When I had to say goodbye
You weren't there to find
You took my fingerprints away
So I would love your mind

I don't pretend to understand
Just what you mean by that
But next time I'll inquire
Before I scratch your back

I wonder if my fingerprints
Get lonely in the crowd
There are no others like them
& that should make them proud

But now you want to marry me
& take me down the aisle
& throw confetti fingerprints
You know that's not my style

Sure I'd like to marry
But I won't face the dawn
With any girl who knew me
When my fingerprints were on

1966

A CROSS DIDN'T FALL ON ME

A cross didn't fall on me
when I went for hot dogs
and the all-night Greek
slave in the Silver Gameland
didn't think I was his brother
Love me because nothing happens

I believe the rain will not
make me feel like a feather
when it comes tonight after
the streetcars have stopped
because my size is definite
Love me because nothing happens

Do you have any idea how
many movies I had to watch
before I knew surely
that I would love you
when the lights woke up
Love me because nothing happens

Here is a headline July 14
in the city of Montreal
Intervention décisive de Pearson
à la conference du Commonwealth
That was yesterday
Love me because nothing happens

Stars and stars and stars
keep it to themselves
Have you ever noticed how private
a wet tree is
a curtain of razor blades
Love me because nothing happens

Why should I be alone
if what I say is true
I confess I mean to find
a passage or forge a passport
or talk a new language
Love me because nothing happens

I confess I meant to grow
wings and lose my mind
I confess that I've
forgotten what for
Why wings and a lost mind
Love me because nothing happens

SONGS OF LEONARD COHEN

SUZANNE

Suzanne takes you down
to her place near the river
you can hear the boats go by
you can spend the night beside her
And you know that she's half crazy
but that's why you want to be there
and she feeds you tea and oranges
that come all the way from China
And just when you mean to tell her
that you have no love to give her
she gets you on her wavelength
and she lets the river answer
that you've always been her lover
    And you want to travel with her
    you want to travel blind
    and you know that she can trust you
    for you've touched her perfect body
    with your mind

And Jesus was a sailor
when he walked upon the water
and he spent a long time watching
from his lonely wooden tower
and when he knew for certain
only drowning men could see him
he said All men will be sailors then
until the sea shall free them
but he himself was broken
long before the sky would open
forsaken, almost human
he sank beneath your wisdom like a stone

And you want to travel with him
you want to travel blind
and you think maybe you'll trust him
for he's touched your perfect body
with his mind

Now Suzanne takes your hand
and she leads you to the river
she is wearing rags and feathers
from Salvation Army counters
And the sun pours down like honey
on our lady of the harbour
And she shows you where to look
among the garbage and the flowers
There are heroes in the seaweed
there are children in the morning
they are leaning out for love
they will lean that way forever
while Suzanne holds the mirror
    And you want to travel with her
    you want to travel blind
    and you know that you can trust her
    for she's touched your perfect body
    with her mind

TEACHERS

I met a woman long ago
Her hair the black that black can go
Are you a teacher of the heart
Soft she answered No

I met a girl across the sea
Her hair the gold that gold can be
Are you a teacher of the heart
Yes but not for thee

I met a man who lost his mind
In some lost place I had to find
Follow me the wise man said
But he walked behind

I walked into a hospital
Where none was sick and none was well
When at night the nurses left
I could not walk at all

Morning came
And then came noon
Dinner time a scalpel blade
Lay beside my spoon

Some girls wander by mistake
Into the mess that scalpels make
Are you the teachers of my heart
We teach old hearts to break

One morning I woke up alone
The hospital and the nurses gone
Have I carved enough, my Lord
Child, you are a bone

I ate and ate and ate
I did not miss a plate
How much do these suppers cost
We'll take it out in hate

I spent my hatred every place
On every work on every face
Someone gave me wishes
And I wished for an embrace

Several girls embraced me, then
I was embraced by men
Is my passion perfect
No, do it once again

I was handsome, I was strong
I knew the words of every song
Did my singing please you
No, the words you sang were wrong

Who is it whom I address
Who takes down what I confess
Are you the teachers of my heart
We teach old hearts to rest

Teachers are my lessons done
I cannot do another one
They laughed and laughed and laughed and said
Well child, are your lessons done
Are your lessons done

WINTER LADY

Travelling lady stay a while
Until the night is over
I'm just a station on your way
I know I'm not your lover

I lived with a child of snow
When I was a soldier
And I fought every man for her
Until the nights grew colder

She used to wear her hair like you
Except when she was sleeping
And then she'd weave it on a loom
Of smoke and gold and breathing

And why are you so quiet now
Standing there in the doorway?
You chose your journey long before
You came upon this highway

Travelling lady stay a while
Until the night is over
I'm just a station on your way
I know I'm not your lover

SO LONG, MARIANNE

Come over to the window, my little darling
I'd like to try to read your palm
I used to think I was some kind of gypsy boy
before I let you take me home

So long, Marianne
it's time that we began
to laugh and cry and cry and laugh
about it all again

You know I love to live with you
but you make me forget so very much
I forget to pray for the angels
and then the angels forget to pray for us

We met when we were almost young
down by the green lilac park
You held on to me like I was a crucifix
as we went kneeling through the dark

Your letters they all say that you're beside me now
Then why do I feel so alone
I'm standing on this ledge and your fine spider web
is fastening my ankle to a stone

Now I need your hidden love
I'm cold as a new razor blade
You left when I told you I was curious
I never said that I was brave

O you are really such a pretty one
I see you've gone and changed your name again
And just when I climbed this whole mountainside
to wash my eyelids in the rain

Your eyes, I forget your eyes
Your body is at home in every sea
How come you gave your news to everyone
when you said it was a secret just for me

So long, Marianne
it's time that we began
to laugh and cry and cry and laugh
about it all again

ONE OF US CANNOT BE WRONG

I lit a thin green candle
to make you jealous of me
but the room just filled up with mosquitoes
they heard that my body was free
Then I took the dust
of a long sleepless night
and I put it in your little shoe
and then I confess
that I tortured the dress
that you wore for the world to look through

I showed my heart to the doctor
He said I'd just have to quit
Then he wrote himself a prescription
Your name was mentioned in it
Then he locked himself
in a library shelf
with the details of our honeymoon
and I hear from the nurse
that he's gotten much worse
and his practice is all in a ruin

I heard of a saint who had loved you
I studied all night in his school
He taught that the duty of lovers
is to tarnish the Golden Rule
And just when I was sure
that his teachings were pure
he drowned himself in the pool
His body is gone
but back here on the lawn
his spirit continues to drool

An Eskimo showed me a movie
he'd recently taken of you
The poor man could hardly stop shivering
His lips and his fingers were blue
I suppose that he froze
when the wind tore off your clothes
and I guess he just never got warm
but you stand there so nice
in your blizzard of ice
Oh please let me come into the storm

HEY, THAT'S NO WAY
TO SAY GOODBYE

I loved you in the morning
Our kisses deep and warm
Your hair upon the pillow
Like a sleepy golden storm
Many loved before us
I know that we are not new
In city and in forest
They smiled like me and you
But now it's come to distances
And both of us must try
Your eyes are soft with sorrow
Hey, that's no way to say goodbye

I'm not looking for another
As I wander in my time
Walk me to the corner
Our steps will always rhyme
You know my love goes with you
As your love stays with me
It's just the way it changes
Like the shoreline and the sea
But let's not talk of love or chains
And things we can't untie
Your eyes are soft with sorrow
Hey, that's no way to say goodbye

I loved you in the morning
Our kisses deep and warm
Your hair upon the pillow
Like a sleepy golden storm
Yes many loved before us
I know that we are not new
In city and in forest
They smiled like me and you
But let's not talk of love or chains
And things we can't untie
Your eyes are soft with sorrow
Hey, that's no way to say goodbye

MASTER SONG

I believe that you heard your master sing
while I lay sick in bed
I believe that he told you everything
that I keep locked away in my head
Your master took you travelling
at least that's what you said
And now do you come back to bring
your prisoner wine and bread?

You met him at some temple
where they take your clothes at the door
he was just some numberless man in a chair
who had just come back from the war
And you wrap up his tired face in your hair
and he hands you the apple core
Then he touches your lips, now so suddenly bare
of all the kisses we put on some time before

And he gave you a German shepherd to walk
with a collar of leather and nails
and he never once made you explain or talk
about all of the little details
such as who had a worm and who had a rock
and who had you through the mails
Now your love is a secret all over the block
and it never stops, not even when your master fails

And he took you up in his aeroplane
which he flew without any hands
and you cruised above the ribbons of rain
that drove the crowds from the stands
Then he killed the lights in a lonely lane
where an ape with angel glands
erased the final wisps of pain
with the music of rubber bands

And now I hear your master sing
You kneel for him to come
His body is a golden string
that your body is hanging from
His body is a golden string
my body has grown numb
Now you hear your master sing
your shirt is all undone

And will you kneel beside this bed
that we polished so long ago
before your master chose instead
to make my bed of snow
Your eyes are wild and your knuckles are red
and you're speaking far too low
No, I can't make out what your master said
before he made you go

And I think you're playing far too rough
for a lady who's been to the moon
I've lain by this window long enough
You get used to an empty room
And your love is some dust in an old man's cuff
who is tapping his foot to a tune
and your thighs are a ruin and you want too much
let's say you came back too soon

I loved your master perfectly
I taught him all that he knew
He was starving in some deep mystery
like a man who is sure what is true
And I sent you to him with my guarantee
I could teach him something new
and I taught him how you would long for me
no matter what he said, no matter what you do

I believe that you heard your master sing
while I lay sick in bed
I suppose that he told you everything
that I keep locked away in my head
Your master took you travelling
(at least, that's what you said)
And now do you come back to bring
your prisoner wine and bread?

SISTERS OF MERCY

All the Sisters of Mercy
they are not departed or gone
They were waiting for me
when I thought that I just can't go on
And they brought me their comfort
and later they brought me this song
Oh I hope you run into them
you who've been travelling so long

You who must leave everything
that you cannot control
It begins with your family
but soon it comes round to your soul
I've been where you're hanging
I think I can see where you're pinned
When you're not feeling holy
your loneliness tells you you've sinned

They lay down beside me
I made my confession to them
They touched both my eyes
and I touched the dew on their hem
If your life is a leaf
that the seasons tear off and condemn
they will bind you with love
that is graceful and green as a stem

When I left they were sleeping
I hope you run into them soon
Don't turn on the light
You can read their address by the moon
And you won't make me jealous
if I hear that they sweetened your night
We weren't lovers like that
and besides it would still be all right

It's true that all the men you knew were dealers who said they were through with dealing every time you gave them shelter. I know that kind of man. It's hard to hold the hand of anyone who's reaching for the sky just to surrender.

And sweeping up the jokers that he left behind you'll find he did not leave you very much not even laughter. Like any dealer he was watching for the card that is so high and wild he'll never need to deal another. He was just some Joseph looking for a manger.

And then leaning on your window-sill he'll say one day you caused his will to weaken with your love and warmth and shelter. And taking from his wallet an old schedule of trains, he'll say, I told you when I came I was a stranger.

But now another stranger seems to want you to ignore his dreams, as though they were the burden of some other. You've seen that man before, his golden arm dispatching cards, but now it's rusted from the elbow to the finger. And he wants to trade the game he plays for shelter. He wants to trade the game he knows for shelter.

You hate to watch another tired man lay down his hand, like he was giving up the Holy Game of Poker. And while he talks his dreams to sleep, you notice there's a highway that is curling up like smoke above his shoulder.

You tell him to come in, sit down, but something makes you turn around. The door is open. You cannot close your shelter. You try the handle of the road. It opens. Do not be afraid. It's you, my love, it's you who are the stranger.

I've been waiting. I was sure we'd meet between the trains we're waiting for, I think it's time to board another. Please understand I never had a secret chart to get me to the heart of this, or any other matter. Well, he talks like this, you don't know what he's after. When he speaks like this, you don't care what he's after.

Let's meet tomorrow if you choose, upon the shore, beneath the bridge, that they are building on some endless river. Then he leaves the platform for the sleeping car that's warm, you realize, he's only advertising one more shelter. And it comes to you, he never was a stranger. And you say, "OK, the bridge, or someplace later."

And then sweeping up the jokers that he left behind, you find he did not leave you very much, not even laughter. Like any dealer he was watching for the card that is so high and wild he'll never need to deal another. He was just some Joseph looking for a manger.

And leaning on your window-sill, he'll say one day you caused his will to weaken with your love and warmth and shelter. And then taking from his wallet an old schedule of trains he'll say, I told you when I came I was a stranger.

SELECTED POEMS
1956–1968

A PERSON WHO EATS MEAT

A person who eats meat
wants to get his teeth into something
A person who does not eat meat
wants to get his teeth into something else
If these thoughts interest you for even a moment
you are lost

MARITA

MARITA
PLEASE FIND ME
I AM ALMOST 30

THIS IS FOR YOU

This is for you
it is my full heart
it is the book I meant to read you
when we were old
Now I am a shadow
I am restless as an empire
You are the woman
who released me
I saw you watching the moon
you did not hesitate
to love me with it
I saw you honouring the windflowers
caught in the rocks
you loved me with them
On the smooth sand
between pebbles and shoreline
you welcomed me into the circle
more than a guest
All this happened
in the truth of time
in the truth of flesh
I saw you with a child
you brought me to his perfume
and his visions
without demand of blood
On so many wooden tables
adorned with food and candles
a thousand sacraments
which you carried in your basket
I visited my clay
I visited my birth

until I became small enough
and frightened enough
to be born again
I wanted you for your beauty
you gave me more than yourself
you shared your beauty
This I only learned tonight
as I recall the mirrors
you walked away from
after you had given them
whatever they claimed
for my initiation
Now I am a shadow
I long for the boundaries
of my wandering
and I move
with the energy of your prayer
and I move
in the direction of your prayer
for you are kneeling
like a bouquet
in a cave of bone
behind my forehead
and I move toward a love
you have dreamed for me

THE REASON I WRITE

The reason I write
is to make something
as beautiful as you are

When I'm with you
I want to be the kind of hero
I wanted to be
when I was seven years old
a perfect man
who kills

YOU DO NOT HAVE TO LOVE ME

You do not have to love me
just because
you are all the women
I have ever wanted
I was born to follow you
every night
while I am still
the many men who love you

I meet you at a table
I take your fist between my hands
in a solemn taxi
I wake up alone
my hand on your absence
in Hotel Discipline

I wrote all these songs for you
I burned red and black candles
shaped like a man and a woman
I married the smoke
of two pyramids of sandalwood
I prayed for you
I prayed that you would love me
and that you would not love me

YOU LIVE LIKE A GOD

You live like a god
somewhere behind the names
I have for you,
your body made of nets
my shadow's tangled in,
your voice perfect and imperfect
like oracle petals
in a herd of daisies.
You honour your own god
with mist and avalanche
but all I have
is your religion of no promises
and monuments falling
like stars on a field
where you said you never slept.
Shaping your fingernails
with a razor blade
and reading the work
like a Book of Proverbs
no man will write for you,
a discarded membrane
of the voice you use
to wrap your silence in
drifts down the gravity between us,
and some machinery
of our daily life
prints an ordinary question in it
like the Lord's Prayer raised
on a rollered penny.
Even before I begin to answer you
I know you won't be listening.

We're together in a room,
it's an evening in October,
no one is writing our history.
Whoever holds us here in the midst of a Law,
I hear him now
I hear him breathing
as he embroiders gorgeously our simple chains.

BEAUTIFUL LOSERS

BE WITH ME

Be with me, religious medals of all kinds, those suspended on silver chains, those pinned to the underwear with a safety pin, those nestling in black chest hair, those which run like tramcars on the creases between the breasts of old happy women, those that by mistake dig into the skin while love is made, those that lie abandoned with cufflinks, those that are fingered like coins and inspected for silver hallmark, those that are lost in clothes by necking fifteen-year-olds, those that are put in the mouth while thinking, those very expensive ones that only thin small girl children are permitted to wear, those hanging in a junk closet along with unknotted neckties, those that are kissed for luck, those that are torn from the neck in anger, those that are stamped, those that are engraved, those that are placed on streetcar tracks for curious alterations, those that are fastened to the felt on the roofs of taxis, be with me as I witness the ordeal of Catherine Tekakwitha.

WHAT IS A SAINT

What is a saint? A saint is someone who has achieved a remote human possibility. It is impossible to say what that possibility is. I think it has something to do with the energy of love. Contact with this energy results in the exercise of a kind of balance in the chaos of existence. A saint does not dissolve the chaos; if he did the world would have changed long ago. I do not think that a saint dissolves the chaos even for himself, for there is something arrogant and warlike in the notion of a man setting the universe in order. It is a kind of balance that is his glory. He rides the drifts like an escaped ski. His course is a caress of the hill. His track is a drawing of the snow in a moment of its particular arrangement with wind and rock. Something in him so loves the world that he gives himself to the laws of gravity and chance. Far from flying with the angels, he traces with the fidelity of a seismograph needle the state of the solid bloody landscape. His house is dangerous and finite, but he is at home in the world. He can love the shapes of human beings, the fine and twisted shapes of the heart. It is good to have among us such men, such balancing monsters of love.

A GREAT FEAST IN QUEBEC

A few days after her baptism Catherine Tekakwitha was invited to a great feast in Quebec. Present were the Marquis de Tracy, the intendant Talon, the Governor M. de Courcelle, the Mohawk Chief Kryn, who was one of the fiercest converts Christianity has ever commanded, and many handsome ladies and gentlemen. Perfume rose out of their hair. They were elegant in the manner only citizens two thousand miles from Paris can be. Wit flourished in every conversation. Butter was not passed without an aphorism. They discussed the activities of the French Academy of Sciences, which was only ten years old. Some of the guests had spring pocket watches, a new timepiece invention which was sweeping Europe. Someone explained another recently developed device used to regulate clocks, the pendulum. Catherine Tekakwitha listened quietly to everything that was said. With a bowed head she received the compliments which the quillwork on her deerskin gown evoked. The long white table shone with the pride of silver and crystal and early spring flowers, and for a minor second her eyes swam in the splendour of the occasion. Handsome servants poured wine into glasses that resembled long-stem roses. A hundred candle flames echoed and re-echoed in a hundred pieces of silver cutlery as the fragrant guests worked over their slabs of meat, and for a minor second the flashing multiple suns hurt her eyes, burned away her appetite. With a tiny abrupt movement which she did not command, she knocked over her glass of wine. She stared at the whale-shaped stain, frozen with shame.

— It is nothing, said the Marquis. It is nothing, child.

Catherine Tekakwitha sat motionless. The Marquis returned to his conversation. It concerned a new military invention which was being developed in France, the bayonet. The stain spread quickly.

— Even the tablecloth is thirsty for this good wine, joked the Marquis. Don't be frightened, child. There are no punishments for spilling a glass of wine.

Despite the suave activity of several servants the stain continued to discolour larger and larger areas of the tablecloth. Conversation dwindled as the diners directed their attention to its remarkable progress. It now claimed the entire tablecloth. Talk ceased altogether as a silver vase turned purple and the pink flowers it contained succumbed to the same influence. A beautiful lady gave out a cry of pain as her fine hand turned purple. A total chromatic metamorphosis took place in a matter of minutes. Wails and oaths resounded through the purple hall as faces, clothes, tapestries, and furniture displayed the same deep shade. Beyond the high windows there were islands of snow glinting in the moonlight. The entire company, servants and masters, had directed its gaze outside, as if to find beyond the contaminated hall some reassurance of a multicoloured universe. Before their eyes these drifts of spring snow darkened into shades of spilled wine, and the moon itself absorbed the imperial hue. Catherine stood up slowly.

— I guess I owe you all an apology.

MAGIC IS ALIVE

Old friend, you may kneel as you read this, for now I come to the sweet burden of my argument. I did not know what I had to tell you, but now I am sure. All my speeches were preface to this, all my exercises but a clearing of my throat. I confess I tortured you but only to draw your attention to this. I confess I betrayed you but only to tap your shoulder. In our kisses and sucks, this, ancient darling, I meant to whisper.

G-d is alive. Magic is afoot. G-d is alive. Magic is afoot. G-d is afoot. Magic is alive. Alive is afoot. Magic never died. G-d never sickened. Many poor men lied. Many sick men lied. Magic never weakened. Magic never hid. Magic always ruled. G-d is afoot. G-d never died. G-d was ruler though his funeral lengthened. Though his mourners thickened. Magic never fled. Though his shrouds were hoisted the naked G-d did live. Though his words were twisted the naked Magic thrived. Though his death was published round and round the world the heart did not believe. Many hurt men wondered. Many struck men bled. Magic never faltered. Magic always led. Many stones were rolled but G-d would not lie down. Many wild men lied. Many fat men listened. Though they offered stones Magic still was fed. Though they locked their coffers G-d was always served. Magic is afoot. G-d rules. Alive is afoot. Alive is in command. Many weak men hungered. Many strong men thrived. Though they boasted solitude G-d was at their side. Nor the dreamer in his cell, nor the captain on the hill. Magic is alive. Though his death was pardoned round and round the world the heart would not believe. Though laws were carved in marble they could not shelter men. Though altars built in parliaments they could not order men. Police arrested Magic and Magic went with them for Magic loves the hungry. But Magic would not tarry. It moves from arm to arm. It would not stay with them. Magic is afoot. It cannot come to harm. It rests in an empty palm. It spawns in an empty mind. But Magic is no instrument. Magic is the end. Many men drove Magic but Magic stayed behind. Many strong men lied. They only passed through Magic and out the other side. Many weak men lied. They came to G-d in secret and though they left him nourished they would not tell who healed. Though mountains danced before them they said that G-d was dead. Though his shrouds were hoisted the naked G-d did live. This I mean to whisper to my mind. This I mean to laugh with in my mind. This I mean my mind to serve till service is but Magic moving through the world, and mind itself is Magic coursing through the flesh, and flesh itself is Magic dancing on a clock, and time itself the Magic Length of G-d.

— All right, Edith. What seems to be the trouble now?

— I can't make myself come any more.

— Of course, you can't. If we're going to perfect the pan-orgasmic body, extend the erogenous zone over the whole fleshy envelope, popularize the Telephone Dance, then we've got to begin by diminishing the tyranny of the nipples, lips, clitoris, and asshole.

— You're going against G-d, F. You say dirty words.

— I'll take my chances.

— I feel so lost since I can't make myself come any more. I'm not ready for the other stuff yet. It makes me too lonely. I feel blurred. Sometimes I forget where my cunt is.

— You make me weary, Edith. To think I've pinned all my hopes on you and your wretched husband.

— Give it back to me, F.

— All right, Edith. It's a very simple matter. We do it with books. I thought this might happen, so I brought the appropriate ones along. I also have in this trunk a number or artificial phalli (used by women), Vaginal Vibrators, the Rin-No-Tam and Godemiche or Dildo.

— Now you're talking.

— Just lie back and listen. Sink into the rubber sheet. Spread your legs and let the air-conditioning do its filthy work.

— O.K., shoot.

I cleared my famous throat. I chose a swollen book, frankly written, which describes various Auto-Erotic practices as indulged in by humans and animals, flowers, children and adults, and women of all ages and cultures. The area covered included: Why Wives Masturbate, What We Can Learn from the Anteater, Unsatisfied Women, Abnormalities and Eroticism, Techniques of Masturbation, Latitude of Females, Genital Shaving, Clitoral

Discovery, Club Masturbation, Female Metal, Nine Rubber, Frame Caress, Urethral Masturbation, Individual Experiments, Masturbation in and of Children, Thigh-Friction Technique, Mammary Stimulation, Auto-Eroticism in Windows.

— Don't stop, F. I feel it coming back.

Her lovely brown fingers inched down her silky rounded belly. I continued reading in my slow, tantalizing, weather-reporting tones. I read to my deep breathing protégée of the unusual sex practices, when Sex Becomes "Different." An "Unusual" sex practice is one where there is some greater pleasure than orgasm through intercourse. Most of these bizarre practices involve a measure of mutilation, shock, voyeurism, pain, or torture. The sex habits of the average person are relatively free of such sadistic or masochistic traits. NEVERTHELESS, the reader will be shocked to see how abnormal are the tastes of the so-called normal person. CASE HISTORIES and intensive fieldwork. Filled with chapters detailing ALL ASPECTS of the sex act. SAMPLE HEADINGS: Rubbing, Seeing, Silk Rings, Satyriasis, Bestiality in Others. The average reader will be surprised to learn how "Unusual" practices are passed along by seemingly innocent, normal sex partners.

— It's so good, F. It's been so long.

Now it was late afternoon. The sky had darkened somewhat. Edith was touching herself everywhere, smelling herself shamelessly. I could hardly keep still myself. The texts had got to me. Goose pimples rose on her young form. I stared dumbly at Original drawings: male and female organs, both external and internal, drawings indicating correct and incorrect methods of penetration. Wives will benefit from seeing how the penis is received.

— Please, F. Don't leave me like this.

My throat was burning with the hunger of it. Love fondled. Edith writhed under her squeezes. She flipped over on her stomach, wielding her small beautiful fists in anal stimulation. I threw myself into a Handbook of Semi-Impotence. There were important pieces woven into the theme: how to enlarge the erect penis, penis darkness, use of lubricants, satisfaction during menstruation, abusing the menopause, a wife's manual assistance in overcoming semi-impotence.

— Don't touch me, F. I'll die.

I blurted out a piece on Fellatio and Cunnilingus Between Brother and Sister, and others. My hands were almost out of control. I stumbled through a new concept for an exciting sex life. I didn't miss the section on longevity. Thrilling culminations possible for all. Lesbians by the hundreds interviewed and bluntly questioned. Some tortured for coy answers. Speak up, you cheap dyke. An outstanding work showing the sex offender at work. Chemicals to get hair off palms. Not models! Actual Photos of Male and Female Sex Organs and Excrement. Explored Kissing. The pages flew. Edith mumbling bad words through froth. Her fingers were bright and glistening, her tongue bruised from the taste of her waters. I spoke the books in everyday terms, the most sensitivity, cause of erection, Husband-Above 1–17, Wife-Above 18–29, Seated 30–34, On-the-Side 35–38, Standing & Kneeling Positions 39–53, Miscellaneous Squats 54–109, Coital Movement in All Directions, both for Husband and Wife.

— Edith! I cried. Let me have Foreplay.

— Never.

I sped through a glossary of Sexual Terms. In 1852, Richard Burton (d. aet. 69) submitted calmly to circumcision at the age of 31. "Milkers." Detailed Library of Consummated Incest. Ten Steps on Miscegenation. Techniques of Notorious Photographers. The Evidence of Extreme Acts. Sadism, Mutilation, Cannibalism, Cannibalism of Oralists, How to Match Disproportionate Organs. See the vivid birth of the new American woman. I shouted the recorded facts. She will not be denied the pleasures of sex. CASE HISTORIES show the changing trends. Filled with accounts of college girls eager to be propositioned. Women no longer inhibited by oral intimacy. Men masturbated to death. Cannibalism during Foreplay. Skull Coition. Secrets of "Timing" the Climax. Foreskin, Pro, Con, and Indifferent. The Intimate Kiss. What are the benefits of sexual experimentation? Own and others' sexual make-up. Sin has to be taught. Kissing Negroes on their Mouths. Thigh Documents. Styles of Manual Pressure in Voluntary Indulgence. Death Rides a Camel. I gave her everything. My voice cried the Latex. I hid no laces, nor a pair of exciting open-front pants, nor soft elasticized bra instead of sagging, heavy wide bust, therefore youthful separation. O'er Edith's separate nipples I blabbed the full record, Santa Pants, Fire Alarm Snow, Glamour Tip, plain wrapper Thick Bust Jelly, washable leather Kinsey Doll, Smegma Discipline, the LITTLE SQUIRT ashtray, "SEND ME ANOTHER Rupture-Easer so I will have one to change off with. It is enabling me to work top speed at my press machine 8 hrs a day," this I threw in for sadness, for melancholy soft flat groin pad which might lurk in Edith's memory swamp as soiled lever, as stretched switch to bumpy apotheosis wet rocket come out of the fine print slum where the only trumpet solo is grandfather's stringy cough and underwear money problems.

Edith was wiggling her saliva-covered kneecaps, bouncing on the rivulets of lubrication. Her thighs were aglow with froth, and her pale anus was excavated by cruel false fingernails. She screamed for deliverance, the flight her imagination commanded denied by a half-enlightened cunt.

— Do something, F. I beg you. But don't touch me.
— Edith, darling! What have I done to you?
— Stand back, F!
— What can I do?
— Try.
— Torture story?
— Anything, F. Hurry.

BELIEVE ME, EDITH

Believe me, Edith, I had to act, and act fast. That was my nature. Call me Dr. Frankenstein with a deadline. I seemed to wake up in the middle of a car accident, limbs strewn everywhere, detached voices screaming for comfort, severed fingers pointing homeward, all the debris withering like sliced cheese out of Cellophane — and all I had in the wrecked world was a needle and thread, so I got down on my knees, I pulled pieces out of the mess and I started to stitch them together. I had an idea of what a man should look like, but it kept changing. I couldn't devote a lifetime to discovering the ideal physique. All I heard was pain, all I saw was mutilation. My needle going so madly, sometimes I found I'd run the thread right through my own flesh and I was joined to one of my own grotesque creations — I'd rip us apart — and then I heard my own voice howling with the others, and I knew that I was also truly part of the disaster. But I also realized that I was not the only one on my knees sewing frantically. There were others like me, making the same monstrous mistakes, driven by the same impure urgency, stitching themselves into the ruined heap, painfully extracting themselves —

— F., you're weeping.

— Forgive me.

— Stop blubbering. See, you've lost your hard-on.

SONGS FROM A ROOM

STORY OF ISAAC

The door it opened slowly,
    my father he came in;
    I was nine years old.
And he stood so tall above me,
    his blue eyes they were shining
    and his voice was very cold.
He said, "I've had a vision
    and you know I'm strong and holy,
    I must do what I've been told."
So we started up the mountain;
    I was running, he was walking,
    and his axe was made of gold.

The trees they got much smaller,
    the lake like a lady's mirror,
    when we stopped to drink some wine.
Then he threw the bottle over,
    I heard it break a minute later,
    and he put his hand on mine.
I thought I saw an eagle
    but it might have been a vulture,
    I never could decide.
Then my father built an altar,
    He looked once behind his shoulder,
    but he knew I would not hide.

You who build these altars now
    to sacrifice the children,
    you must not do it any more.
A scheme is not a vision
    and you never have been tempted
    by a demon or a god.
You who stand above them now,
    your hatchets blunt and bloody,
    you were not there before:
when I lay upon a mountain
    and my father's hand was trembling
    with the beauty of the word.

And if you call me Brother now,
    forgive me if I enquire:
    Just according to whose plan?
When it all comes down to dust,
    I will kill you I if must,
    I'll help you if I can.
When it all comes down to dust,
    I will help you if I must,
    I'll kill you if I can.
And mercy on our uniform,
    man of peace, man of war —
    the peacock spreads his fan!

LADY MIDNIGHT

I came by myself to a very crowded place. I was looking for someone who had lines in her face. I found her there, but she was past all concern. I asked her to hold me; I said: Lady, unfold me, but she scorned me and told me I was dead and could never return.

I argued all night, like so many have before, saying: Whatever you give me, I need so much more. Then she pointed at me where I kneeled on the floor. She said: Don't try to use me, or slyly refuse me, just win me or lose me — it is this that the darkness is for!

I cried, O Lady Midnight, I fear that you grow old; the stars eat your body and the wind makes you cold. If we cry now, she said, it will only be ignored. So I walked through the morning, the sweet early morning, I could hear my lady calling: You've won me, you've won me, my lord.

YOU KNOW WHO I AM

I cannot follow you my love
You cannot follow me
I am the distance you put between
All of the moments that we will be

You know who I am
You've stared at the sun
I am the one who loves changing
from nothing to one

Sometimes I need you naked
Sometimes I need you wild
I need you to carry my children in
I need you to kill a child

If you should ever track me down
I will surrender there
And I'll leave with you one broken man
Whom I will teach you to repair

You know who I am
You've stared at the sun
I am the one who loves changing
from nothing to one

SEEMS SO LONG AGO, NANCY

It seems so long ago, Nancy was alone. Looking at the Late Late Show through a semi-precious stone. In the House of Honesty her father was on trial. In the House of Mystery there was no one at all. *There was no one at all.*

It seems so long ago, none of us were strong. Nancy wore green stockings and she slept with everyone. She never said she'd wait for us although she was alone. I think she fell in love for us in nineteen sixty-one. *Nineteen sixty-one.*

It seems so long ago, Nancy was alone. A forty-five beside her head, an open telephone. We told her she was beautiful. We told her she was free. But none of us would meet her in the House of Mystery. *The House of Mystery.*

And now you look around you. See her everywhere. Many use her body. Many comb her hair. And in the hollow of the night when you are cold and numb, you hear her talking freely then. She's happy that you've come. *She's happy that you've come.*

BIRD ON THE WIRE

Like a bird on the wire
Like a drunk in a midnight choir
I have tried in my way to be free
Like a worm on a hook
Like a knight from some old-fashioned book
I have saved all my ribbons for thee
If I have been unkind
I hope that you can just let it go by
If I have been untrue
I hope you know it was never to you

Like a baby stillborn
Like a beast with his horn
I have torn everyone who reached out for me
But I swear by this song
And by all that I have done wrong
I will make it all up to thee
I saw a beggar leaning on his wooden crutch
He said to me "You must not ask for so much"
And a pretty woman leaning in her darkened door
She cried to me "Hey, why not ask for more"

Like a bird on the wire
Like a drunk in a midnight choir
I have tried in my way to be free

SONGS OF LOVE AND HATE

JOAN OF ARC

Now the flames they followed Joan of Arc
as she came riding through the dark,
no moon to keep her armour bright,
no man to get her through this smoky night
She said, "I'm tired of the war,
I want the kind of work I had before:
a wedding dress or something white
to wear upon my swollen appetite."

"I'm glad to hear you talk this way
I've watched you riding every day,
and something in me yearns to win
such a cold and very lonesome heroine."
"And who are you?" she sternly spoke,
to the one beneath the smoke.
"Why, I'm fire," he replied,
"and I love your solitude, I love your pride."

"Then fire make your body cold,
I'm going to give you mine to hold."
And saying this she climbed inside
to be his one, to be his only bride.
And deep into his fiery heart
he took the dust of Joan of Arc,
and high above the wedding guests
he hung the ashes of her wedding dress.

It was deep into his fiery heart
he took the dust of Joan of Arc,
and then she clearly understood
if he was fire, oh, then she was wood.
I saw her wince, I saw her cry
I saw the glory in her eye
Myself, I long for love and light,
but must it come so cruel, must it be so bright!

AVALANCHE

I stepped into an avalanche
it covered up my soul
When I am not this hunchback
I sleep beneath a golden hill
You who wish to conquer pain
you must learn to serve me well

You strike my side by accident
as you go down for gold
The cripple that you clothe and feed
is neither starved nor cold
He does not ask for company
not at the centre of the world

When I am on this pedestal
you did not raise me there
Your laws do not compel me
to kneel grotesque and bare
I myself am the pedestal
for this hump at which you stare

You who wish to conquer pain
you must learn what makes me kind
The crumbs of love that you offer me
are the crumbs I've left behind
Your cross is no credential here
it's just the shadow of my wound

I have begun to long for you
I who have no need
I have begun to wait for you
I who have no greed
You say you've gone away from me
but I can feel you when you breathe

Do not dress in rags for me
I know you are not poor
And don't love me quite so fiercely
when you know you are not sure
It is your world beloved
it is your flesh that I wear

DIAMONDS IN THE MINE

The woman in blue
she's asking for revenge
The man in white (that's you)
says he has no friends
The river is swollen up
with dirty rusty cans
and the trees are burning
in your promised land

And there are no letters
in the mailbox
there are no grapes
upon the vine
there are no chocolates
in your boxes any more
and there are no diamonds
in the mine

You tell me that your lover
has a broken limb
You say you're restless now
and it's on account of him
I saw the man in question
it was just the other night
He was eating up a lady
where the lions and Christians fight

And there are no letters

There is no comfort
in the covens of the witch
Some very clever doctor went
and sterilized the bitch
And the only man of energy
(the revolution's pride)
showed a million women
how to kill an unborn child

And there are no letters
in the mailbox
there are no grapes
upon the vine
there are no chocolates
in your boxes any more
and there are no diamonds
in the mine

FAMOUS BLUE RAINCOAT

It's four in the morning, the end of December. I'm writing you now just to see if you're better. New York is cold but I like where I'm living. There's music on Clinton Street all though the evening. I hear that you're building your little house deep in the desert. You're living for nothing now. I hope you're keeping some kind of record. *Yes, and Jane came by with a lock of your hair. She said that you gave it to her the night that you planned to go clear. Did you ever go clear?*

The last time we saw you you looked so much older. Your famous blue raincoat was torn at the shoulder. You'd been to the station to meet every train but then you came home without Lili Marlene. And you treated my woman to a flake of your life. And when she came back she was nobody's wife. *I see you there with a rose in your teeth, one more thin gypsy thief. Well, I see Jane's awake. She sends her regards.*

And what can I tell you my brother my killer? What can I possibly say? I guess that I miss you. I guess I forgive you. I'm glad that you stood in my way. If you ever come by here for Jane or for me, I want you to know that your enemy is sleeping. I want you to know that his woman is free. *Yes, and thanks for the trouble you took from her eyes. I thought it was there for good, so I never tried.*

And Jane came by with a lock of your hair. She said that you gave it to her that night that you planned to go clear.

Sincerely, L. Cohen.

THE ENERGY OF SLAVES

WELCOME TO THESE LINES

Welcome to these lines
There is a war on
but I'll try to make you comfortable
Don't follow my conversation
it's just nervousness
Didn't I make love to you
when we were students of the East
Yes the house is different
the village will be taken soon
I've removed whatever
might give comfort to the enemy
We are alone
until the times change
and those who have been betrayed
come back like pilgrims to this moment
when we did not yield
when we steadfastly refused
to call the darkness poetry

THE ONLY POEM

This is the only poem
I can read
I am the only one
can write it
I didn't kill myself
when things went wrong
I didn't turn
to drugs or teaching
I tried to sleep
but when I couldn't sleep
I learned to write
I learned to write
what might be read
on nights like this
by one like me

PORTRAIT OF A GIRL

She sits behind the wooden shutters
on a very hot day
The room is dark, the photographs gloomy
She is profoundly worried
that her thighs are too big
and her ass fat and ugly
Also she is too hairy
The lucky American girls are not hairy
She sweats too much
There is a fine mist caught
on the darks hairs above her mouth
I wish I could show her
what such hair and haunches
do for one like me
Unfortunately I don't know who she is
or where she lives
or if indeed she lives at all
There is no information about this person
except in these lines
and let me make it clear
as far as I'm concerned
she has no problem whatsoever

I PERCEIVED THE OUTLINE OF YOUR BREASTS

I perceived the outline of your breasts
through your Hallowe'en costume
I knew you were falling in love with me
because no other man could perceive
the advance of your bosom into his imagination
It was a rupture of your unusual modesty
for me and me alone
through which you impressed upon my shapeless hunger
the incomparable and final outline of your breasts
like two deep fossil shells
which remained all night long and probably forever

THE ESCAPE

O darling (as we used to say)
you are wide-hipped and kind
I'm glad we got over the wall
of that loathsome Zen monastery
We are not exactly young
but there is still some pleasure
to be squeezed from these leather bags
Even as we lie here in Acapulco
not quite in each other's arms
several young monks walk single-file
through the snow on Mount Baldy
shivering and farting in the moonlight:
there are passages in their meditation
that treat our love and wish us well

I AM DYING

I am dying
    because you have not
died for me
    and the world
still loves you

I write this because I know
that your kisses
    are born blind
on the songs that touch you

I don't want a purpose
    in your life
I want to be lost among
      your thoughts
the way you listen to New York City
when you fall asleep

1967

I know there's no such thing
      as hell or heaven
I know it's 1967
but are you sleeping have you slept
with any of my friends
It's not just something I want to know
it's the only thing I want to know
not about the mystery of G-d
not about myself
and am I the beautiful one
The only wisdom I want to have
is to know if I am
or if I am not alone in your love

UGLY IN MY OWN EYES

Whenever I happen to see you
I forget for a while
that I am ugly in my own eyes
for not winning you

I wanted you to choose me
over all the men you know
    because I am destroyed
in their company

I have often prayed for you
like this
    Let me have her

THERE ARE NO TRAITORS

There are no traitors among women
Even the mother does not tell the son
they do not wish us well

She cannot be tamed by conversation
Absence is the only weapon
against the supreme arsenal of her body

She reserves a special contempt
for the slaves of beauty
She lets them watch her die

Forgive me, partisans,
I only sing this for the ones
who do not care who wins the war

I LEFT A WOMAN

I left a woman waiting
I met her sometime later
she said, Your eyes are dead
what happened to you, lover

And since she spoke the truth to me
I tried to answer truly
Whatever happened to my eyes
happened to your beauty

O go to sleep my faithful wife
I told her rather cruelly
Whatever happened to my eyes
happened to your beauty

INVISIBLE TONIGHT

I am invisible tonight
Only certain shy women see me
All my hideous days of visibility
I longed for their smiles
Now they lean out of their shabby
plans-for-the-evening
so we may salute one another
Sisters of mine
of my own shattered people
going after third-choice lovers
they smile at me to indicate
that we can never meet
as long as we permit
this order of things to persist
in which we are the wretched ones

LOVE IS A FIRE

Love is a fire
It burns everyone
It disfigures everyone
It is the world's excuse
for being ugly

YOU TORE YOUR SHIRT

You tore your shirt
to show me where
you had been hurt
I had to stare

I put my hand
on what I saw
I drew it back
It was a claw

Your skin is cured
You sew your shirt
You throw me food
and change my dirt

THREAT

This is a threat
Do you know what a threat is
I have no private life
You will commit suicide
or become like me

DARK AT FOUR O'CLOCK

It gets dark at four o'clock now
The windshield is filled with night and cold
the motor running for the heater's sake
We finally forgive ourselves
and touch each other between the legs
At last I can feel the element of welcome in our kisses

FAR FROM THE SOIL

Terez and Deanne elude me
Terez and Deanne
   that is how great a poet I am

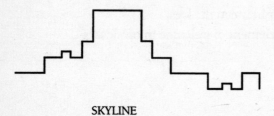

SKYLINE

and artist too
  I could grow to love
the fucking in New York
  far from the soil
but dreamy and courageous

MY ROOM

Come down to my room
I was thinking about you
and I made a pass at myself

THE ROAD TO LARISSA

I was lost
when I met you on the road
to Larissa
the straight road between the cedars

You thought
I was a man of roads
and you loved me for being such a man
I was not such a man

I was lost when
I met you on the road
to Larissa

I AM PUNISHED

I am punished when I do not sweat
or when I try to invent something
I am one of the slaves
You are employees
That is why I hate your work

AQUARIAN AGE

Welcome to this book of slaves
which I wrote during your exile
you lucky son-of-a-bitch —
while I had to contend
with all the flabby liars
of the Aquarian Age

THE KILLERS

The killers that run
       the other countries
are trying to get us
to overthrow the killers
       that run our own
I for one
prefer the rule
       of our native killers
I am convinced
       the foreign killer
will kill more of us
than the old familiar killer does
       Frankly I don't believe
anyone out there
really wants us to solve
our social problems
       I base this all on how I feel
about the man next door
I just hope he doesn't
       get any uglier
Therefore I am a patriot
I don't like to see
       a burning flag
because it excites
the killers on either side
to unfortunate excess
which goes on gaily
       quite unchecked
until everyone is dead

PUREST OF OCCASIONS

His suicide was simply not a puzzle
especially to those of us
who photographed him
with his mouth open
behind a grime of dots

We saw him meeting a girl
quite by accident
the blue night of the estate
upheld by lemon trees
resembling small-faced orchestras

We stood by on the rim
of a bullet hole looking down
as he laced her huge new boot
with a boa constrictor

Sing for him, Leonard,
your love of honey qualifies you
to wear his raincoat
and his stinging shaving lotion
for this purest of occasions

YOU WENT TO WORK

You went to work at the U.N.
and you became a spy
for a South American government
because you cared for nothing
and you spoke Spanish
That was several years after we made love
in the honey air of autumn Montreal:
Athens was beautiful in the old days
the drugstores were free
We knew ten great cities by heart
Death to the Powers
who have destroyed the style of travel
Let them stutter their bland secrets
over your long legs and tall fingers
Let them have your wooden love
Death to the Vanguard
Death to the Junta
Death to the Passport Control

ANY SYSTEM

Any system you contrive without us
will be brought down
We warned you before
and nothing that you built has stood
Hear it as you lean over your blueprint
Hear it as you roll up your sleeve
Hear it once again
Any system you contrive without us
will be brought down
You have your drugs
You have your guns
You have your Pyramids your Pentagons
With all your grass and bullets
you cannot hunt us any more
All that we disclose of ourselves forever
is this warning
Nothing that you built has stood
Any system you contrive without us
will be brought down

ONE OF THESE DAYS

One of these days
you will be the object
of the contempt of slaves
Then you will not talk so easily
about our freedom and our love
Then you will refrain
from offering us your solutions
You have many things on your mind
We think only of revenge

I TRY TO KEEP IN TOUCH

I try to keep in touch wherever I am
I don't say I love you
I don't say I worked it out
The sun comes in the skylight
My work calls to me
sweet as the sound of the creek
beside the cabin in Tennessee
I listen at my desk
and I am almost ready to forgive
the ones who tried to crush us
with their fine systems
Your beauty is everywhere
which we distilled together
out of the hard times

You will never feel me leading you
Forever I escape your homage
I have no ideas to shackle you
I have nothing in mind for you
I have no prayers to put you in
I live for you
without the memory of what you deserve
or what you do not deserve

MY GREED

It is not to tell you anything
but to live forever
that I write this
It is my greed that you love
I have kept nothing for myself
I have despised every honour
Imperial and mysterious
my greed has made a slave of you

YOUR EYES

Your eyes are very strong
They try to cripple me
You put all your strength
into your eyes
because you do not know
how to be a hero

You have mistaken your ideal
It is not a hero
but a tyrant
you long to become
Therefore weakness
is your most attractive quality

I have no plans for you
Your dangerous black eyes
fasten on the nearest girl
or the nearest mirror
as you go hopefully
from profession to profession

THIS IS WAR

There is no one
to show these poems to
Do not call a friend to witness
what you must do alone
These are my ashes
I do not intend to save you any work
by keeping silent
You are not yet as strong as I am
You believe me
but I do not believe you
This is war
You are here to be destroyed

I'D LIKE TO READ

I'd like to read
one of the poems
that drove me into poetry
I can't remember one line
or where to look

The same thing
happened with money
girls and late evenings of talk

Where are the poems
that led me away
from everything I loved

to stand here
naked with the thought of finding thee

THE POEMS DON'T LOVE US ANY MORE

The poems don't love us any more
they don't want to love us
they don't want to be poems
Do not summon us, they say
We can't help you any longer

There's no more fishing
in the Big Hearted River
Leave us alone
We are becoming something new

They have gone back into the world
to be with the ones
who labour with their total bodies
who have no plans for the world
They never were entertainers

I live on a river in Miami
under conditions I cannot describe
I see them sometimes
half-rotted half-born
surrounding a muscle
like a rolled-up sleeve
lying down in their jelly
to make love with the tooth of a saw

STAY

Stay
    stay a little longer
timid shadow
        of my repose
      fastened so lightly
        to the breath before
            my first question

Thou art the hunger
can disarm
        every appetite

What embrace
    satisfies the child
who will not kill?

ETIQUETTE

The Ark you're building
in your yard
Will you let me on
Will you let me off
Don't you think
we all should study Etiquette
before we study Magic

N.Y., 1967

A VEIL

There was a veil between them
composed of good thread
not carelessly woven

Therefore they did not ignore it
or poke at it, but honoured
what hid them, one from the other

Thus they served their love
as those old Spanish masters served
The One Who Does Not Manifest

A FUTURE NIGHT

Dipped myself in a future night
like a long-armed candle-maker
Came back too gross for love
Useless as I seem in my coat of greed
I will have an unborn woman
when I am only print

MOROCCO

I brought a man his dinner
He did not wish to look into my eyes
He ate in peace

SONG FOR MY ASSASSIN

We were chosen, we were chosen
miles and miles apart:
I to love your kingdom
you to love my heart.

The love is intermittent
the discipline continues
I work on your spirit
you work on my sinews.

I watch myself from where you are:
do not be mistaken:
the spider web you see me through
is the view I've always taken.

Begin the ceremony now
that we have been preparing:
I'm tired of this marble floor
that we have both been sharing.

THE WRONG MAN

They locked up a man
who wanted to rule the world
The fools
They locked up the wrong man

ONE

One of the lizards
was blowing bubbles
as it did pushups on the tree trunk
I did pushups this morning
on the carpet
and I blew bubbles of Bazooka
last night in the car
I believe the mystics are right
when they say we are all One

THIS IS MY VOICE

This is my voice
but I am only whispering
The amazing vulgarity
of your style
invites men to think
of torturing you to death
but I am only whispering
The ocean is whispering
The junk-yard is whispering
We no longer wish to learn
what you know how to do
There is no envy left
If you understood this
you would begin to shiver
but I am only whispering
to my tomahawk
so that the image itself
may reduce you to scorn
and weaken you further

NEW SKIN FOR THE OLD CEREMONY

CHELSEA HOTEL

I remember you well in the Chelsea Hotel,
you were talking so brave and so sweet;
   giving me head on the unmade bed,
while the limousines wait in the street.
   And those were the reasons, and that was New York,
we were running for the money and the flesh;
   and that was called love for the workers in song,
probably still is for those of them left.

   But you got away, didn't you, baby,
you just turned your back on the crowd.
   You got away, I never once heard you say:
"I need you, I don't need you,
I need you, I don't need you," —
   and all of that jiving around.

I remember you well in the Chelsea Hotel,
you were famous, your heart was a legend.
   You told me again you preferred handsome men,
but for me you would make an exception.
   And clenching your fist for the ones like us
who are oppressed by the figures of beauty,
   you fixed yourself, you said: "Well, never mind,
we are ugly, but we have the music."

   But you got away, didn't you, baby,
you just threw it all to the ground.
   You got away, I never once heard you say:
"I need you, I don't need you,
I need you, I don't need you," —
   and all of that jiving around.

I don't mean to suggest that I loved you the best;
I don't keep track of each fallen robin.
I remember you well in the Chelsea Hotel —
that's all, I don't even think of you that often.

TAKE THIS LONGING

Many men have loved the bells
you fastened to the rain;
and everyone who wanted you,
they found what they
will always want again —
your beauty lost to you yourself,
just as it was lost to them —

Take this longing from my tongue,
all the useless things
my hands have done;
let me see your beauty broken down,
like you would do
for one you love.

Your body like a searchlight.
My poverty revealed.
I would like to try your charity,
until you cry:
"Now you must try my greed."
And everything depends upon
how near you sleep to me —

Take this longing from my tongue,
all the lonely things
my hands have done;
let me see your beauty broken down,
like you would do
for one you love.

Hungry as an archway
through which the troops have passed,
I stand in ruins behind you
with your winter clothes,
your broken sandal strap.
But I love to see you naked there.
especially from the back —

Take this longing from my tongue,
whatever useless things
these hands have done;
untie for me your high blue gown,
like you would do
for one you love.

You're faithful to the better man.
Well, I'm afraid that he left.
So let me judge your love affair
in this very room where I have
sentenced mine to death.
I'll even wear these old laurel leaves
that he's shaken from his head —

Take this longing from my tongue,
all the useless things
these hands have done;
let me see your beauty broken down,
like you would do
for one you love.

FIELD COMMANDER COHEN

Field Commander Cohen, he was our most important spy, wounded in the line of duty, parachuting acid into diplomatic cocktail parties, urging Fidel Castro to abandon fields and castles, leave it all, and, like a man, come back to nothing special, such as waiting rooms, and ticket lines, and silver bullet suicides, and messianic ocean tides, and racial roller-coaster rides, and other forms of boredom advertised as poetry. *I know you need your sleep now, I know your life's been hard, but many men are falling where you promised to stand guard.*

I never asked but I heard you cast your lot along with the poor. How come I overheard your prayer that you be this and nothing more than just some grateful, faithful woman's favourite singing millionaire, the patron saint of envy and the grocer of despair, working for the Yankee dollar? *I know you need your sleep now, I know your life's been hard, but many men are falling where you promised to stand guard.*

Lover, come and lie with me, if my lover is who you are. And be your sweetest self a while, until I ask for more, my child. Then let the other selves be rung, yes, let them manifest and come 'til every taste is on the tongue, 'til love is pierced and love is hung, and every kind of freedom done, then *oh my love, oh my love, oh my love, oh my love.*

THERE IS A WAR

There is a war between the rich and poor, a war between the man and the woman. There is a war between the ones who say "there is a war" and the ones who say "there isn't." *Why don't you come on back to the war? It's just beginning.*

I live here with a woman and a child. The situation makes me kind of nervous. I rise up from her arms, she says, "I guess you call this love. I call it Room Service." *Why don't you come on back to the war? Don't be a tourist. Why don't you come on back to the war? Let's all get nervous.*

You cannot stand what I've become, you much prefer the gentleman I was before. I was so easy to defeat. I was so easy to control. I didn't even know there was a war. *Why don't you come on back to the war? Don't be embarrassed. Why don't you come on back to the war? You can still get married.*

There is a war between the rich and poor, a war between the man and the woman. There is a war between the left and right, a war between the black and white, a war between the odd and the even. *Why don't you come on back to the war? Take up your tiny burden. Why don't you come on back to the war? It's just beginning. Why don't you come on back to the war? Let's all get even.*

IS THIS WHAT YOU WANTED

You were the promise at dawn
I was the morning after
You were Jesus Christ, my Lord
I was the money-lender
You were the sensitive woman
I was Sigmund Freud
You were the manual orgasm
I was the dirty little boy

And is this what you wanted
to live in a house that is haunted
by the ghost of you and me?

You were Marlon Brando
I was Steve McQueen
You were KY Jelly
I was Vaseline
You were the Father of Modern Medicine
I was Mr. Clean
You were the Whore and the Beast of Babylon
I was Rin Tin Tin

And is this what you wanted
to live in a house that is haunted
by the ghost of you and me?

You got old and wrinkled
I stayed seventeen
You lusted after many
I stayed here with one
You betrayed your solitude
I came through alone
You said that you could never love me
I undid your gown

And is this what you wanted
to live in a house that is haunted
by the ghost of you and me?

WHY DON'T YOU TRY

Why don't you try to do without him, why don't you try to live alone? Do you really need his hands for your passion? Do you really need his heart for your throne? Do you need his labour for your baby? Do you need his beast for the bone? Do you need to hold a leash to be a lady? I know that you can make it, you can make it on your own.

Why don't you try to forget him? Just open up your dainty little hand? You know, this life is filled with many sweet companions, many satisfying one-night stands. Do you want to be the ditch around a tower? Do you want to be the moonlight in his cave? Do you want to give your blessings to his power as he goes whistling past his daddy, past his daddy's grave?

I'd like to take you to the ceremony; that is, if I remember the way. Jack and Jill, they're going to join their misery; I'm afraid it's time for everyone to pray. You can see they've finally taken cover. They're willing, they're willing to obey. Their vows are difficult, they're for each other. So let nobody put a loophole, put a loophole in their way.

I TRIED TO LEAVE YOU

I tried to leave you. I don't deny. I closed the book on us at least a hundred times. I'd wake up every morning by your side.

The years go by. You lose your pride. The baby's crying so you do not go outside. And all your work is right before your eyes.

Goodnight, my darling. I hope you're satisfied. The bed is kind of narrow, but my arms are open wide. And here's a man still working for your smile.

WHO BY FIRE?

Who by fire? Who by water? Who in the sunshine? Who in the
night time? Who by high ordeal? Who by common trial? Who in
your merry, merry month of May? Who by very slow decay? *And
who shall I say is calling?*

Who in her lonely slip? Who by barbiturate? Who in these
realms of love? Who by something blunt? Who by avalanche?
Who by powder? Who for his greed? Who for his hunger? *And
who shall I say is calling?*

Who by brave ascent? Who by accident? Who in solitude? Who
in this mirror? Who by his lady's command? Who by his own
hand? Who in mortal chains? Who in power? *And who shall I say
is calling?*

A SINGER MUST DIE

The courtroom is quiet, but who will confess? Is it true you betrayed us? The answer is Yes. Then read me the list of the crimes that are mine. I will ask for the mercy that you love to decline. *And all the ladies go moist, and the judge has no choice: a singer must die for the lie in his voice.*

I thank you, I thank you for doing your duty, you keepers of Truth, you guardians of Beauty. Your vision is right. My vision is wrong. I'm sorry for smudging the air with my song. *La la la la la la, la la la la la la*

The night it is thick, and my defences are hid in the clothes of a woman I would like to forgive; in the rings of her silk, in the hinge of her thighs, where I had to go begging in beauty's disguise. *Goodnight, goodnight, my night after night, my night after night after night after night*

I am so afraid, I listen to you. Your sun-glassed protectors they do that to you. It's their ways to detain, it's their ways to disgrace, their knee in your balls and their fist in your face. *Yes, and long live the state! By whoever it's made! Sir, I didn't see nothing, I was just getting home late.*

And save me a place in the twelve-dollar grave
with those who took money for the pleasure they
gave; with those always ready, with those who
undressed so you could lay down with your head
on somebody's breast. *And all the ladies go moist,*
and the judge has no choice: a singer must die for the
lie in his voice.

DEATH OF A LADIES' MAN

MEMORIES

Frankie Laine was singing "Jezebel"
I pinned an Iron Cross to my lapel
I walked up to the tallest
    and the blondest girl
I said, "Look, you don't know me now
    but very soon you will;
so won't you let me see,
won't you let me see,
won't you let me see your naked body?"

She said, "Just dance me
to the dark side of the gym
Chances are,
    I'll let you do most anything
I know you're hungry
    I can hear it in your voice
and there are many parts of me to touch
    you have your choice.
But no, you cannot see,
no, you cannot see,
no, you cannot see my naked body."

We're dancing close,
the band is playing "Stardust"
Balloons and paper streamers
    floating down on us
She says, "You've got a minute left
    to fall in love."
In solemn moments such as this
    I've put my trust
and all my faith to see,
all my faith to see,
all my faith to see her naked body.

PAPER-THIN HOTEL

The walls of this hotel are paper-thin
Last night I heard you
 making love to him
The struggle mouth to mouth
 and limb to limb
The grunt of unity when he came in

I stood there with my ear
 against the wall
I was not seized by jealousy at all
In fact a burden lifted from my soul
I heard that love
 was out of my control
A heavy burden lifted from my soul
I learned that love
 was out of my control

I listened to your kisses at the door
I never heard the world
so close before
You ran your bath and you began to sing
I felt so good I couldn't feel a thing

I can't wait to tell you to your face
I can't wait for you to take my place
You are The Naked Woman
 In My Heart
You are The Angel
 With Her Legs Apart
It's written on the walls of this hotel
You go to heaven once
 you've been to hell

A heavy burden lifted from my soul
I heard that love
    was out of my control

TRUE LOVE LEAVES NO TRACES

As the mist leaves no scar
On the dark green hill
So my body leaves no scar
On you and never will

Through windows in the dark
The children come, the children go
Like arrows with no target
Like shackles made of snow

True love leaves no traces
If you and I are one
It's lost in our embraces
Like stars against the sun

As a falling leaf may rest
A moment in the air
So your head upon my breast
So my hand upon your hair

And many nights endure
Without a moon, without a star
So will we endure
When one is gone and far

True love leaves no traces
If you and I are one
It's lost in our embraces
Like stars against the sun

I LEFT A WOMAN WAITING

I left a woman waiting.
I met her sometime later.
She said, *I see your eyes are dead.*
What happened to you, lover?
What happened to you, my lover?

And since she spoke the truth to me
I tried to answer truthfully:
Whatever happened to my eyes
Happened to your beauty
What happened to your beauty
Happened to me.

We took ourselves to someone's bed
And there we fell together
Quick as dogs and truly dead were we
And free as running water
Free as running water
Free as you and me
The way it's got to be, lover
The way it's got to be.

DON'T GO HOME WITH YOUR HARD-ON

I was born in a beauty salon
My father was a dresser of hair
My mother was a girl you could call on
When you called she was always there

But don't go home with your hard-on
It will only drive you insane
You can't shake it (or break it)
  with your Motown
You can't melt it down in the rain

I've looked behind all of these faces
That smile you down to your knees
And the lips that say, come on, taste us
And when you try to, they make you say Please

Here comes your bride with her veil on
Approach her, you wretch, if you dare
Approach her, you ape, with your tail on
Once you have her she'll always be there

So I work in that same beauty salon
I'm chained to the old masquerade
The lipstick, the shadow and the silicone
I follow my father's trade

But don't go home with your hard-on
It will only drive you insane
You can't shake it (or break it)
  with your Motown
You can't melt it down in the rain

DEATH OF A LADY'S MAN

I KNELT BESIDE A STREAM

I knelt beside a stream which was manifesting on a polished wooden floor in an apartment above Central Park. A feathered shield was fastened to my left forearm. A feathered helmet was lowered on my head. I was invested with a duty to protect the orphan and the widow. This made me feel so good I climbed on Alexandra's double bed and wept in a general way for the fate of men. Then I followed her into the bathroom. She appeared to turn gold. She stood before me as huge as the guardian of a harbour. How had I ever thought of mastering her? With a hand of chrome and an immense Gauloise cigarette she suggested that I give up and worship her, which I did for ten years. Thus began the obscene silence of my career as a lady's man.

THE CAFÉ

The beauty of my table.
The cracked marble top.
A brown-haired girl ten tables away.
Come with me.
I want to talk.
I've taken a drug that makes me want to talk.

COMMENTARY — THE CAFÉ

The notebooks indicate that this café was situated near the waterfront in the part of Piraeus. I could not find it. Upon inquiry, I discovered that it had been demolished and the marble tabletops thrown into the harbour. The brunette, who was thin, then, is now a skeleton. Her sleeveless summer frock is for sale on Deluth Street on a wire hanger. The little cardboard boxes of Maxiton, the flat sliding metal containers of Ritalin, quite absent from self-service pharmacies. The pretty conversation dissolved immediately into the sunlight which is why it was urgent and breathless. Standing on the quay, I saw some ghostly shapes in the depths but I was told they were sunken Javex bottles.

THE CHANGE

I could not trade you for a nightingale. I could not trade you
for a hammered golden bird. You took away my music. You set me
here with blunted tongue to listen only. Someone is playing a
grand piano with two hands. Someone is whispering to her
shepherd. I never got to wear my high leather boots. I never
became a sign for everything that is high and nervous. You
entered me into a quarrel with a woman and you said, This is your
voice. You put the moon in a microscope. You dimmed the beauty
of everything that is not her and then you dimmed her beauty. I
never got to build the barn. Only once did I ride with Kid Marley.
Someone is squeezing the old accordion. They are performing the
national dance. The patriots have gathered round. O sir, you were
so beautiful as a woman. You were so beautiful as a song. You are
so ugly as a god.

COMMENTARY — THE CHANGE

*I think this qualifies as great religious poetry and also earns itself
a place in the annals of complaint. The boots come from Clarence, an
aluminum-fronted boutique on the Champs-Elysees. Kid Marley was
a rodeo champion from Tennessee who sold the author a lame horse in
the late sixties.*

DEATH TO THIS BOOK

Death to this book or fuck this book and fuck this marriage. Fuck the twenty-six letters of my cowardice. Fuck you for breaking the mirror and throwing the eyebrow tweezers out the window. Your dead bed night after night and nothing warm but baby talk. Fuck marriage and theology and the cold goodnight. Fuck the idolatry of anger and the priests who say so. How dare they. How dare they. Thanks for your judgement on me. Murder and a fast train to Paris and me thin again in my blue raincoat, and Barbara waiting at the Cluny Square Hotel. Fuck her for never turning up.

COMMENTARY — DEATH TO THIS BOOK

There hasn't been a book like this in a long time. The modern reader will be provided a framework of defeat through which he may view without intimidation a triumph of blazing genius. I have the manuscript beside me now. It took him years to write. During this time you were all grinding out your bullshit. It will become clear that he is the stylist of his era and the only honest man in town. He did not quarrel with his voices. He took it down out of the air. This is called work by those who know and should not be confused with an Eastern trance.

ANOTHER ROOM

I climbed the stairs with my key and my brown leather bag and I entered room eight. I heard Aleece mounting the steps behind me. Room eight. My own room in a warm country. A bed, a table, a chair. Perhaps I could become a poet again. Aleece was making noises in the hall. I could see the ocean in the late afternoon light outside the window. I should look at the ocean but I don't feel like it. The interior voice said, You will only sing again if you give up lechery. Choose. This is a place where you may begin again. But I want her. Let me have her. Throw yourself upon your stiffness and take up your pen.

She makes a noise in the hallway
Come in, I say
She comes in
Out to the balcony
Stand behind her
Lean over, I say
Up with her skirt
Drool in my hand
to open it up
Watch the sunset
over her hair
Are you connected
to the hotel, the chambermaid perhaps? I say
No, I'm the one
you are writing about, she says
the one who sails down
the pillars of blood
from brain to isthmus
and lost in your unhanded trousers
I cause myself to come true

How noble I felt after writing these lines. Aleece had gone away. The emanations of my labour had cleared the hallway. And how much more satisfying this concentration than trifling with a foreign presence or, worse, disturbing another's heart.

COMMENTARY — ANOTHER ROOM

But you have *disturbed my heart. Even if my legs are made of stainless steel and a fish circles in the air at the height of my buttocks I am not protected from your agitation of my heart. I am a bee in your world. I am a squirrel. I move too quickly. I die too fast. Your song is cruel and selfish. You have no gasp to express me. I smell so wonderfully sea-like. There is a seaweed bandage, a one-layered seaweed bandage, on something torn in me. It is futile to contact you in the midst of your training but I've been hoping you might fall on a spear and leave your master and live with me on the servicemen's beach behind the Gad Hotel. My legs have been in a jukebox ever since you left. I am Dutch, I am young, I have sailed the world. Bring the fish back to my anus and bring the bee back to your swollen bite. And remember me, Green Eyes, remember your shell-shocked whore and the lather of her ruthless shaving. I appeared in this world with you when you were lost in the pride of being alone. I took you to bath and I took you to bed and I put sand in your mouth by the ocean.*

Forgive me, Aleece, forgive me *is scrawled across the seascape pictured on this giant postcard.*

DEATH OF A LADY'S MAN

The man she wanted all her life
　　was hanging by a thread.
"I never even knew how much
　　I wanted you," she said.
His muscles they were numbered
　　and his style was obsolete.
"O baby, I have come too late."
　　She knelt beside his feet.

"I'll never see a face like yours
　　in years of men to come,
I'll never see such arms again
　　in wrestling or in love."
And all his virtues burning
　　in this smoky holocaust,
she took unto herself
　　most everything her lover lost.

Now the master of this landscape
　　he was standing at the view
with a sparrow of St. Francis
　　that he was preaching to.
She beckoned to the sentry
　　of his high religious mood.
She said, "I'll make a space between my legs,
　　I'll teach you solitude."

He offered her an orgy
    in a many-mirrored room;
he promised her protection
    for the issue of her womb.
She moved her body hard
    against a sharpened metal spoon,
she stopped the bloody rituals
    of passage to the moon.

She took his much-admired
    oriental frame of mind,
and the heart-of-darkness alibi
    his money hides behind.
She took his blonde madonna
    and his monastery wine.
"This mental space is occupied
    and everything is mine."

He tried to make a final stand
    beside the railway track.
She said, "The art of longing's over
    and it's never coming back."
She took his tavern parliament,
    his cap, his cocky dance;
she mocked his female fashions
    and his working-class moustache.

The last time that I saw him
    he was trying hard to get
a woman's eduction
    but he's not a woman yet.
And the last time that I saw her
    she was living with a boy
who gives her soul an empty room
    and gives her body joy.

So the great affair is over
    but whoever would have guessed
it would leave us all so vacant
    and so deeply unimpressed.
It's like our visit to the moon
    or to that other star:
I guess you go for nothing
    if you really want to go that far.

MY WIFE AND I

My wife and I made love this afternoon. We hid together from the light of our desire, forehead to forehead. Later she asked me, Did I taste sweet for you? Dear companion, you did. This evening I watched with pleasure as she undressed and put on her flannel pyjamas. I held her closely until she went to sleep. Then I closed the light and left the room carefully and I came down here to you.

COMMENTARY — MY WIFE AND I

Who can go beyond the first four words? Who can hurry past the final six?

Poet of the two great intimacies, you have appeared again to unify our grave concerns.

Where is she now? Where are these flannel pyjamas? Where is your tenderness to Woman and to G-d?

I know you are cheating somewhere; nevertheless, I consent to be profoundly touched by the exquisite accident of this paragraph.

I did not have this work in mind as a child, but I am not ashamed to be your exegete.

THE NEWS YOU REALLY HATE

You fucking whore, I thought that you were really interested in music. I thought your heart was somewhat sorrowful. I might have gone with you under the desk and eaten a soft-boiled egg. I'm going to tell my baby brother not to do what I have done. I'm going to tune you until the string breaks. The Communists do not know how evil you really are.

We are different from you. That's the news you really hate. That's the news to ring the bells and start the fires while your boyfriend serves you the hairball lunch. I have been admitted through the stained-glass shadows where your stench is unwelcome. How dare you pay us any attention? I'm going to eat now. I have declared war on you forever and ever. Disguised as a hat I will rip off your eyebrows. I am going to be here in the sun for a long time. The fragrance comes up again. It does not reach you. It does not invite you to close your eyes in the storm. The trumpets cry up inside me and my king is home. I am judged again with mercy.

COMMENTARY — THE NEWS YOU REALLY HATE

It is sometimes refreshing to embrace a position of uncompromising unforgiveness. As the poet shows, there are surprises and rewards that follow in the wake of the undiluted expression of one's hateful seizures.

However, if you are unskilled in the subtle transformative processes of language, it is best not to write down your ugly thoughts. If you must, do not show them to one who has the power to transmute. He will not be able to help you. He cannot recover from what he himself has begun.

I DECIDED

I decided to jump literature ahead a few years. Because you are angry, I decided to infuriate you. I am infected with the delirious poison of contempt when I rub my huge nose into your lives and your works. I learned contempt from you. Philistine implies a vigour which you do not have. This paragraph cannot be seized by an iron fist. It is understood immediately. It recoils from your love. It has enjoyed your company. My work is alive.

THE BEETLE

Do not be frightened. Where is the beetle I gave you? It is a companion for you somewhere in the room. Here is my peace. These tears will help you. I placed you at a table in the middle of the night. I let you move toward your pain. I let you come near. I let you come in. Now you have no names for yourself. Now you are my creature. This is the mercy. These are the clean tears. You may speak to me now. I will not take your work from you. Have you tired of my mercy? Have you wept enough? Have you seized an image of me? This is the voice of one turning aside. This is my holy work. It has changed the world since you began this word and you are still reading the instructions. Where is your beetle? It pleased you not to want to murder it. An oath of friendship between you and your beetle came to your lips. It was touching. You are the beetle I do not crush, so busy in the light of my eyes. This is the room I prepared for you. It is here you will prepare the marriage. You will untarnish it. You will sweep the chamber where I form my worlds. Now you may have back your stone heart. Someone walks by your window, a slight limp in his step. You cannot see outside and this is my world also. Come to me again when you are not tired, when your panic makes you alert to me, and the perfection of my world bends you down in shame.

COMMENTARY — THE BEETLE

Is there a modern reader that can measure up to this page? Is there one quiet enough? Is there one who has prepared herself? Is there a wall in Los Angeles on which such a beetle could appear?

I have been sitting still for two hours in a cabin on a mountain. The crickets give a pulse to the night. A fly bangs around inside my lampshade. His book lies open before me but I do not know how to approach the purity of this passage.

In all the scriptures of the West, has G-d ever spoken so gently?

THE ALTAR

There is a certain power in his book that cannot be denied even though you try to deny it in every word. Deny it here. Am I less disgusting than you are? Am I happier? Near the beginning of the Bible I am told how to build the Altar. It is to be raised with unhewn stones. You are such a sad hewer of stones. And you are an amusing enemy. Especially when you discover for us all your standards of hewn stone. You may worship here. You can rip a heart out on this paragraph.

COMMENTARY — THE ALTAR

There are many hearts baking on this altar. There is the heart behind the beautiful brown nipple that would not erect itself. There is the heart of one who tried to follow in my footsteps when I had stopped moving. There is the heart of one high above me who stooped to become my rival. There is the heart of the idolator who said that G-d was love alone. My maid's heart is there, who served me too long. There is the heart that did not believe in the stone knife. There is the heart that envied and the heart that surrendered to the anonymity of this miracle. Among these few that I have offered there is my own, the heart of a translator who has tried to render into common usage the high commands of pure energy, who has not denied his own inclination to obey. If these hearts of mine are badly carved it is because THE ALTAR seduced me into a mood of happy careless butchery.

THIS MARRIAGE

I said, Because it is so horrible between us I will go and stop Egypt's bullet. She said, That's beautiful. Then I can commit suicide and the child falls into strangers' hands. Great, I said. Yug, yug, yug, she said. What you did to me, I said. The lonely, we said. The nights of hands on ourselves. Your unkindness, we said. Your greed. Your unkindness. Your bitter tongue. Give me time. You never learn. Your ancestors. My ancestors. Fuck you, I said. You shit. Stop screaming. I can't stand it. You can't stand anything. Nobody can live like this. In front of the child. Let him learn. This is no good. Yer fuckin right it's no good. This kitchen was once beautiful. Oil lamps, order, the set table. Sabbath observed. That's what I want. You don't want it. You don't know what I want. You don't know anything about me. You never did. Not in the beginning. Not now.

In the realms where this marriage was sealed, where the wedding feast goes on and on, where Adam and Eve face one another, the foundations are faultless and secure, your beast's hair flares like black fire upward and your breasts, now in maidenhood, now in motherhood, draw down my face, our hunger blessed by sun and moon, a ring of dancers round the house where within the room is hid, where within the bed is undone, whereupon the hunger's joined, where within the hunger speaks precise instructions to the chosen ones who cannot leave each other.

COMMENTARY — THIS MARRIAGE

This marriage is locked. It is impossible to enter. It is a marriage and operates like one, healing itself the moment it is condemned. In every house there is this marriage which cannot be explained. In our day it appears fragile and easily violated, but it is still the profoundest initiation, and one into which no stranger can intrude.

COMMENTARY II — THIS MARRIAGE

He hangs a crown over his filthy kitchen and expects us to put our hands together and say Grace.

THE PHOTOGRAPH

My dark companion photographs me among the daisies.
My life in art.
She is beautiful when she smiles.
She should smile more often.
We have the same nature.
We are lazy and fascinating.
One day we will go back to that creek in Tennessee
and she will shoot me with a .22.
Take one with my hat on.
We have lots of film.
I taught her how to greet a man in the morning.
These things have been lost
like the arch and the goldenrods.
She asked me to teach them to her —
forgotten modes I happen to remember.
I told her about the time
Adam and Eve tried to commit suicide
but unformed infants of the Milky Way
raised a house against them.
Some of the daisies are up to my thigh.
It is very bright.
The daisies shine back at the sun.
The wind polishes the air.
Some fool might try to pick out a lamentation.
Take one of us together.

IT'S PROBABLY SPRING

So-and-so is sick of all the shit but doesn't feel that bad today because it's probably Spring. The laundry in the sunshine tells the obscene family story of power and love but it doesn't matter because it's probably Spring. Jack is fat and Jane is twisted from the Plague. But you don't have to choose today because it's probably Spring. You're nothing like the pilot, nothing like the matador, you're nothing like the one I waited for, but I won't rub your nose into everything you haven't done because it's probably Spring. I can listen to the bugle now, I can stand beside the old windmill, I can think about my loyal dog buried in the snow. Sally lost her fragrance and her broken heart won't show but she's going to bite her lip and start again because it's finally Spring. The little lambs are leaping through the Easter hoop so the insomniac can get to sleep but he's caught without his knife and fork because it's probably Spring. It's probably Spring. You can give away your money for an hour. You can resume your childhood plan. You're naked and the snake is hungry but the vicious thing won't sting because it's probably Spring. All the poison clouds have settled in a thimble which you nearly make me drink but then you smash it in the fireplace because it's probably Spring. But let's be quiet so we can hear the naval band. They're fine looking lads and they're playing the National Hymn. Their sweat is sweet beneath the woollen uniforms, it's hot and scratchy but they'll be in white tomorrow because of it's being probably Spring. It is the passion of our Lord. It is the ladder through her hair. It is a lovely field which you cannot find in the city. It is what you can never find again so tender and so wild, so do kneel down and honour what the Name makes manifest because it's probably Spring. O stand in due respect for that which flings your wife into another's arms, which heaves the poppy shrapnel through your heart, which invites you to forgive some shabby crime you're likely to commit because it's probably Spring.

I would like to lose my faith in this poet, but I can't. I would like to say that I have discovered in him something glib. I want to disqualify him. He comes too close to betraying me. He comes too close to reeling me in. I want to say that he was too rich. I want to prove that his marriage was happy. I want to say that I only thought he was that good because I misunderstood him. But I am afraid I do not misunderstand him. I understand him. Tonight I understand him perfectly as I sit here heavy with Chinese food under the royal-blue sky of the Los Angeles night, with very little going for me (as they say down here), with much gone sour, but never mind, I do not know how to begin to earn your attention. There is a mood for which Beethoven is too loud, and Bach too wise, and silence too good for a filthy heart such as beats in my breast, but I take my comfort from the creaky hurdy-gurdy tune cranked out uselessly by the one I follow morning and night on a whim of love and a gambler's chance. I read the piece again and again, so pleased that the poet has taken such pains not to touch me. If only I had touched her this lightly, I might not be sitting here now.

ANOTHER FAMILY

Sister in the snow, I took another family
and you did not, I took two children out of my knee.
Your brother has fallen down to be cold again —
on his palm he offers two small figures to the white storm

I couldn't get away, I took another childhood,
I broke my promise not to go back, and it's cold.
I broke my promise not to suffer, and now
I have to start all over again to earn my solitude

Your mistake is elegant, mine is clumsy,
my scarf is wet and I can't think about myself.
Please be proud of your crystal, your well-made crystal
which does not leak and where you don't shiver

You can be no one and I must be my father,
haunting another childhood with my panic,
and I was meant to be frozen beside you, frozen upright
above the goldfish in the solid silver waterfall

and I have to forget what I hate, I have already
begun to forget, it is not hatred any more, it is
the old childhood, my father's heart attack,
and long instructions about my buttons and my shoes

I left my lover to sit at the head of the table.
My wife has to wonder where I've been
and I have to explain that she was wrong, I was
never strong, I was merely frozen with my sunlight in the ice

Now you are alone, you are truly alone,
you were the one who remained standing,
and I betrayed the ending, I fell down under the big snowflakes
just like my father, just like his father

and I don't care about anyone again, they can all
go to hell, it is the only luxury down here
where everything changes into nothing new, and you
wait to be cut down in revenge by your duplicate

THE ASTHMATIC

Because you will not overthrow your life. You cannot breathe. Because of the panic of homelessness. You cannot breathe. Because you have begun to worship time. You cannot breathe. Because you will never have the beautiful one. You cannot breathe. You cannot breathe. Because your sorrow will not return to its birthplace. You cannot breathe. Because you believe you were not meant to be so far away. You cannot breathe. Because this is the valley of the shadow of death. You cannot breathe. Because you cannot be here.

Because you do not know what is coming. You cannot breathe. Because this world is yours and it is not yours. You cannot breathe. Because you rest, because you strive, because you do not work. You cannot breathe. Because you let the world come between you and me. You cannot breathe. Because of an idea of the calm breath. You cannot breathe. Because you want to choose a way. You cannot breathe. Because you find the language to welcome me. You cannot breathe. The sun is sparkling all over the blue water. The stony shore is laved by the sea. Yellow curtains are sucked against the portholes. The propeller wants everyone to go to sleep. You separate yourself from an unknown woman in a green sweater. Because of your love of conquering. You cannot breathe. Because you will not address me as an equal. Because you have commanded the guards to shut down the doors and take away breathing. Because the world is stamped with order, like a seal in formless wax. Because you have a G-d of justice. Because the justice is immediate and flawless. You cannot breathe. Because you cannot uphold your separation. Because your strangerhood is defeated. Because you breathe your breath through the mask of purity. Because you consign to the pale of objectivity her green sweater, the flashing island, your distance from love, and your whole breathless predicament. You cannot breathe.

Exposure to this page can induce a suffocating attack in those who are prone to express the condition of profound indecision which asthma probably is. These sinister rhythms betray the quack and we behold the subversive and imperial intention of a mind that wishes to enslave existence in the name of sweet salvation. Here is the old weapon disguised as charity; greed disguised as the usual prayer, and his trap of panic as an invitation to self-reform. I have begun to turn against this man and against this book.

A WOMAN'S DECISION

Even though you outwit me, I'm not going back to you. Even though the purity of your love is affirmed by the unanimous quiver of every feather in the celestial host, I am not going back to the axe of your love, O triumphant husbandman and lasso king of the gateless horses, I am not going back to you, even though I squirm in your arms and surrender to your will the total essence of my dusty shell here in this captured sweat-hall, I am never coming back, I swear by the rent curtain of my virginity and the blood-thick silence between the bridgeless worlds, that I will lie to you forever, and I will be never again the cup of your need.

I BURY MY GIRLFRIEND

You ask me how I write. This is how I write. I get rid of the lizard. I eschew the philosopher's stone. I bury my girlfriend. I remove my personality from the line so that I am permitted to use the first person as often as I wish without offending my appetite for modesty. Then I resign. I do errands for my mother, or someone like her. I eat too much. I blame those closest to me for ruining my talent. Then you come to me. The joyous news is mine.

A DIFFERENT DRUM

When it comes to lamentations
I prefer Aretha Franklin
to, let's say, Leonard Cohen
Needless to add, he hears a different drum

A WORKING MAN

I had a wife and children
I got drunk on Saturday night
I went to work every day
I hated the rich
I wanted to fuck a college girl
I was proud to be a working man
I hated the assholes
      who run the revolution
The ones like me will win
We do not need words
You are all on your knees
      looking for the lost nipple
We stand here
We are already above you
Soon the law will be ours
Soon you will experience our mercy
I have no friends
I have no class
There is no we
I had to play on your social illusions
      to get you here in the middle of the night
Dip your flags in the blood
Light your torches
The women are waiting
      in high-buttoned white dresses
Your dignity is restored

COMMENTARY — A WORKING MAN

We don't give a shit about all this so don't try to threaten us with hints of a New Order. The beings that hover round this table have already overthrown the World and shoved it back up your asshole exactly the same as it was before.

THE UNCLEAN START

I went down to the port with my wife. On the way down I accused her of continuing her relentless automatic assault on the centre of my being. I knew this was not wise. I only meant to rap her on the knuckles and direct her attention to her habitual drift toward bitchiness but I lost control. There is no control in these realms. I became a thug. I attacked her spirit. Her spirit armed itself and retaliated massively. I think we were talking about valises or which of us travelled the lightest. A truce was investigated briefly by shabby deputies neither of which had the authority to begin the initiative. You always carry something extra, a shopping bag, something of string and paper that can't be checked. I'm glad you didn't pack for me. You always slow me down. I can't be an acrobat when you're around. You're sand-paper. I can't be a dancer. I'm dead when you're around. You kill. It is your nature. Observe your nature. The shoemaker looked up at us as we passed his open doorway. This humiliation made me furious. I shoved a razor blade into her nerves. Her eyes changed colour. This was done by saying Jesus Christ, quickening my step slightly, minutely moving my jaw, rejecting the essence of her totally and forever. If she went down quickly I would nurse her back to love in time to get her blessings before the boat came in. But why should I, she didn't rub my back when I threw my shoulder out, even when I asked her three times. And why should she since I had defeated her smile over and over. And why should I since she was the enemy of my freedom and the smiling moon over my gradual death. And why should she since I hated her because her beauty died. Why should I because there must be a woman in Jerusalem or beside me on the airplane. Half asleep Old John saw us but it was no humiliation since he didn't recognize me any more and I no longer greeted him. Captain Mad Body saw us but it didn't matter because he was mute and crazy and lived on the port and knew the shames of everyone. We were on the port, in plain sunlight between the masts and the shops. The shit piled up in the One Heart which is the engine of our energy. We are married: there is only one heart. On common ground the armoured spirits tried to embrace but they both fell down paralyzed. Pain removed the world. They felt for the organs of sex but they were gone. There was no war, no peace, no world, the punishment of marriage spoiled. There is no Armageddon here. And fuck you. And fuck you. The horn, the boat was coming. I would have to travel without her blessing in the collapsed world. I won't accuse you of ruining my trip. I won't accuse you of ruining your absence. The *Kamelia* came in, its white decks above us, or was it the *Portokalios Ilios*. I know the name of a boat or two. I always hide her beauty from myself until it is too late to praise her for it. Ropes were flying, uniforms flashing, everywhere haste advised and the threat of lost time. I stared at her as she became beautiful and calm. I would not get the blessing. The journey had an unclean start. And she must carry stillborn blessings up the hill.

ANGELICA

Angelica stands by the sea
Anything I say is too loud for her mood
I will have to come back
a million years later
with the scalp of my old life
hanging from one hand

THE NEXT ONE

Things are better in Milan.
Things are a lot better in Milan.
My adventure has sweetened.
I met a girl and a poet.
One of them was dead
    and one of them was alive.
The poet was from Peru
    and the girl was a doctor.
She was taking antibiotics.
I will never forget her.
She took me into a dark church
    consecrated to Mary.
Long live the horses and the candles.
The poet gave me back my spirit
    which I had lost in prayer.
He was a great man out of the civil war.
He said his death was in my hands
because I was the next one
    to explain the weakness of love.
The poet Cesar Vallejo
    who lies at the foot of his forehead.
Be with me now great warrior
whose strength depends solely
    on the favours of a woman.

A MARVELLOUS WOMAN

a marvellous night
a marvellous woman
they married in the winter
they parted in the spring
she threw her wedding ring
into the Lake of Decisions
she continued
he continued
they met again
in the south of France
she was living alone
but in great beauty
he appeared to her
as a toad
she chased him
out of the 18th century
he thinks of her all the time
but in the winter
he goes crazy
he walks up & down the room
singing Hank Williams
the police put tickets on his car
the snow removal people
cover it with snow
finally it is towed away
to a huge white field
of frozen dogs

THE EVENT

The event engrossed me.
A pigeon flew across the window.
The Chinese girl smiled.
I made my vows to her.
We would never fuck.
We would never speak.
We would never meet.
The unlimited grey afternoon
supported all its creatures evenly.

YOU HAVE NO FORM

You have no form, you move among, yet do
not move, the relics of exhausted thought
of which you are not made, but which give world to
you, who are of nothing made, nothing wrought.
There you long for one who is not me, O
queen of no subject, newer than the morning,
more antique than first seed dropped below
the wash where you are called and Adam born.
And here, not your essence, not your absence
weds the emptiness which is never me,
though these motions and these formless events
are preparation for humanity,
and I get up to love and eat and kill
not by my own, but by our married will.

THE DREAM

O I had such a wonderful dream, she said.
I dreamed you made love to me.
At last, he said to himself, the spirit
has taken up some of the heavy work.

I LIKE THE WAY YOU OPPOSED ME

I like the way you opposed me when you thought I had fallen into silence. You were so happy that I had nothing to teach you, and nobody spoke of my exploits. All this depended on a curious belief of yours that there was only one stage, and you had been waiting for my piece to end, feeling so ripe and swollen for the spot. And here I am again, with the news of another freedom, just when yours was selling well and the competition was under control. You might like to know what my wife said to me upstairs. She's wearing her wine bikini, she's rather attractive, you know, in spite of her shaved head which was the idea of your Central Committee. She said, Leonard, whenever you leave the room an orange bird comes to the window.

BESIDE MY SON

I lay beside my sleeping son.
He was not a child now.
A dream radiated from his lips.
He was unusually good company.

COMMENTARY — BESIDE MY SON

May you bless the union of your mother and father
May you discard easily the husks of my thought
May you stand on my dead body

SHE HAS GIVEN ME THE BULLET

Just after sunset
waves creeping up to our toes
my wife said: I have everything I want
I looked down at her hair
as she snuggled against my shoulder like a rifle-butt
Toward the horizon
mist fumed out of the water changing clearly
into the eternal shapes of comfort and ordeal
I will bring these down, I said to myself,
she has given me the bullet

COMMENTARY — SHE HAS GIVEN ME THE BULLET

There is the bullet but there is no death. There is the mist but there is no death. There is the embrace but there is no death. There is the sunset but there is no death. There is the rotting and the hatred and the ambition but there is no death. There is no death in this book and therefore it is a lie.

THE GOOD FIGHT

If only she'd call me Mister again
If only my genitals didn't float
When I relaxed in the bath
And we both looked down and we both agreed
It's stupid to be a man
Don't tell my mother I've become
The appendix of a full-grown woman
I'm made of her I'm useless to her
I'm something gouged out with her beauty
I'm the shape of her perfume
I'm the chime of wire hangers
That she took her clothes down from
When I made her strong and angry
With the subtlest insults I could devise
And still she would not fall
And I knew for certain
She was the Magnum Opus of my middle age

THE DOVE

I saw the dove come down, the dove with the green twig, the childish dove out of the storm and flood. It came toward me in the style of the Holy Spirit descending. I had been sitting in a café for twenty-five years waiting for this vision. It hovered over the great quarrel. I surrendered to the iron laws of the moral universe which make a boredom out of everything desired. Do not surrender, said the dove. I have come to make a nest in your shoe. I want your step to be light.

THE ROSE

I was never bothered by the rose. Some people talk about it all the time. It fades, it blooms. They see it in visions, they have it, they miss it. I made some small efforts to worry about the rose but they never amounted to much. I don't think you should do those things to a flower. They don't exist anyhow. The garden doesn't exist either. Believe me, these things stand in the way. I was with a man when he actually saw the rose. He said his mother was standing at the centre of it. I went to war with the rose on my banner but I didn't fight very well. The rose has never eluded me. It's the most natural thing to see it burning in the air in front of me like a little fire in the middle of a sheet of paper, a bright hole with blackened edges. Sometimes it floats over my shoulder like a red umbrella. It has four green leaves at the cardinal points. It claims to sponsor these lines. It is a very modest claim but it stands in the way. It was granted to me to discard the authority of the rose. Between the cheeks it still has its terrors. These are harmless conventions. I smell the fragrance. It has even filled up my car on the highway far from any flower bed. I can feel the thorns if I want to move my hand that carelessly. All this is perfectly natural. Sometimes the rose occupies the opening of the far end of a tunnel. I never allow this to dignify my approach. They are continually hovering in windows and other apertures which attract light or desire. They are usually perceived one at a time and while the petals may undulate the centre is still. I never greet the rose and I never ask it to represent an idea or a woman. I find this stands in the way. Everywhere I discover men speaking to the rose. It does not improve their ordinary conversation. Then there is the wound like a rose. This is a particularly nauseating conception. The rose-wound. The petals are made of blood and the energy is made of pain. One of these dwells under my white shirt. There are three roses in my room right now and another trying to establish me as its centre. These are interfering dreams. Don't trouble yourself to brush them aside. You wouldn't know how to do it anyway, and they would probably install themselves on the floor near your feet in theatrical attitudes of agony and neglect.

NOT GOING BACK

It's been hard since I left The Garden
I don't feel so good in my clothes
But I'm not shaking hands with The Warden
And I'm not going back to The Rose

I miss the vice of a man like Christ
And there's too many Arthur Rimbauds
But I'm not going back to Paradise
And I'm not going back to The Rose

MONTREAL

Beware of what comes out of Montreal, especially during winter. It is a force corrosive to all human institutions. It will bring everything down. It will defeat itself. It will establish the wilderness in which the Brightness will manifest again.

We who belong to this city have never left The Church. The Jews are in The Church as they are in the snow. The most violent atheist radical defectors from le Parti Québécois are in The Church. Every style in Montreal is the style of The Church. The winter is in The Church. The Sun Life building is in The Church. Long ago the Catholic Church became a pebble beside the rock on which The Church was founded. The Church has used the winter to break us and now that we are broken we are going to pull down your pride. The pride of Canada and the pride of Quebec, the pride of the left and the pride of the right, the pride of muscle and the pride of heart, the insane pride of your particular vision will swell and explode because you have all dared to think of killing people. The Church despises your tiny works of death and The Church declares that EVERY MAN, WOMAN AND CHILD IS PROTECTED.

FRENCH AND ENGLISH

I think you are fools to speak French
It is a language which invites the mind
to rebel against itself causing inflamed ideas
grotesque postures and a theoretical approach
to common body functions. It ordains the soul
in a tacky priesthood devoted to the salvation
of a failed erection. It is the language
of cancer as it annexes the spirit and
installs a tumour in every honeycomb
Between the rotten teeth of French are incubated
the pettiest notions of destiny and the shabbiest
versions of glory and the dreariest dogma of change
ever to pollute the simplicity of human action
French is a carnival mirror in which the
brachycephalic idiot is affirmed and encouraged
to compose a manifesto on the destruction of the sideshow

I think you are fools to speak English
I know what you are thinking when you speak English
You are thinking piggy English thoughts
you sterilized swine of a language that has no genitals
You are peepee and kaka and nothing else
and therefore the lovers die in all your songs
You can't fool me you cradle of urine
where Jesus Christ was finally put to sleep
and even the bowels of Satan cannot find
a decent place to stink in your flat rhythms
of ambition and disease
English, I know you, you are frightened by saliva
your adventure is the glass bricks of sociology
you are German with a licence to kill

I hate you but it is not in English
I love you but it is not in French
I speak to the devil but it is not about your punishment
I speak to the table but it is not about your plan
I kneel between the legs of the moon
in a vehicle of perfect stuttering
and you dare to interview me on the matter
of your loathsome destinies
you poor boobies of the north
who have set out for heaven with your mouths on fire
Surrender now surrender to each other
your loveliest useless aspects
and live with me in this and other voices
like the wind harps you were meant to be
Come and sleep in the mother tongue
and be awakened by a virgin
(O dead-hearted turds of particular speech)
be awakened by a virgin
into a sovereign state of common grace

O WIFE UNMASKED

O wife unmasked
O body of my plunder
foundation of my waiting
unforgivable
and continually alluring
Some witness loves you
as you blunder through
the webs of my sleeping spirit
Some witness points at our bed
like a monument to romance and song
and gets another crowd to wonder
O juices and fragrance
and inhospitable warmth
O last remains of dignity
O shadow brood of hatred love remorse
O ribbons and trajectories
annulling distances
O wires and rays and chains
What channels of intense air
trembling to a signal
What alloys of eyesore and starlight
What sad bureaucracy of luck
to be with you and you alone
muddling through the Day of Judgement

THE WINDOW

A blond boy wearing thick glasses just looked in my window, or rather at my window, for he used it as a mirror in which he confirmed his coiffure and his expression. I was afraid he might catch sight of me behind his reflection but he quit his work unaware of the self-centred host of this sunken room, and I did not have to confront him in the midst of his vanity.

YOUR DEATH

You are a dead man
writing me a letter
Your sunglasses are beside you
on the square table
on the green felt
You write carefully
sentence after sentence
to make your meaning clear
The meaning is
that you are dead
dead with hope
dead with spring
dead with the blurred hummingbird
dead with the longing
to shine again
in details of the past
And you are tied to your death
with hope
with the hope of sliding out
from under your death
and then to stand
and brandish a scar
in the palm of your hand
like an invitation to the next ordeal
You pass the night
with the source of your death
trying to praise it
trying to sell it
trying to touch it
Your death is fine with me
It has given you

the beautiful head you wanted
the face with good lines
and even though
you cannot inhabit this skull
I can and I do
and I thank you
for the deep heroism
of your useless correspondence

PETITIONS

The blind man loves you with his eyes, the deaf man with his music. The hospital, the battlefield, the torture room, serve you with numberless petitions. On this most ordinary night, so bearable, so plentiful in grave distractions, touch this worthless ink, this work of shame. Inform me from the great height of your beauty.

THE REBELLION

It was a terrible rebellion
I rebelled against a sentence
    between her legs
I punished myself with a holiday
I took a ghost to bed
and caught the seed in the palm of my hand
Her green cotton dress was pulled up
She sat on my face all night long
She dragged me to Jerusalem
and married me over and over
while the silver star of Bethlehem
coughed and spat
in a smoker's reveille
and the priesthood forced me to resume
my old domestic conversation

THE PRICE OF THIS BOOK

I had high hopes for this book. I used to be thin, too. I thought I might live in one place and know one woman. I walked through the starlight this morning. I made my way through the lambs to the slanted concrete floor. I had on my red apron and I had the woman I loved. I wanted to end it, but it would not end: my life in art. I had pledged my deepest health to work this out. The working was way beyond this book. I see this now. I am ashamed to ask for your money. Not that you have not paid more for less. You have. You do. But I need it to keep my different lives apart. Otherwise I will be crushed when they join, and I will end my life in art, which a terror will not let me do.

ROSHI

Roshi poured me a glass of Courvoisier. We were in the cabin on Mt. Baldy, summer of 1977. We were listening to the crickets.

— Kone, Roshi said, you should write cricket poem.

— I've already written a cricket poem. It was in this cabin two years ago.

— Oh.

Roshi fried some sliced pork in sunflower oil and boiled a three-minute noodle soup. We finished one bottle of Courvoisier and opened another.

— Yah, Kone, you should write cricket poem.

— That is a very Japanese idea, Roshi.

— So.

We listened to the crickets a while longer. Then we closed the light so we could open the door and get the breeze without the flies coming in.

— Yah. Cricket.

— Roshi, give me your idea of a cricket poem.

— Ha, ha. Okay:

> dark night (said Roshi)
> cricket sound break out
> cricket girlfriend listening

— That's pretty good, Roshi.

> — dark night (Roshi began again)
> walking on the path
> suddenly break out cricket sound
> where is my lover?

— I don't like that one.

— cricket! cricket! (Roshi cried)
  you are my lover
  now I am walking path by alone
  but I am not lonely with you

— I'm afraid not, Roshi. The first one was good.

Then the crickets stopped for a while and Roshi poured the Courvoisier into our glasses. It was a peaceful night.

— Yah, Kone, said Roshi very softly. You should write more sad.

THIS WRETCH

I'm fucking the dead people now
not you with your breast on fire
not you with your blouse on the floor

Why do you ring the bell in the night
as if we lived in a town
as if the infant were born
as if the Mystery survived

I'm fucking the dead people now
I don't have to try for a song
I don't have to count up to ten

Why did you let your fingers grow
Why do you wear your jeans so round
There's snow on your eye. Your underwear
is cold especially the rim

Not waiting for a parachute
Don't want to scrape off the moon
Try to die on your stomach
I'm fucking the dead people now

HURRY TO YOUR DINNER

Hurry to your dinner. Hurry to your food. Finish the feeble prayer, your stonework, your golem duties to the woman being born. Hurry to the thigh on the plate and the cloudy city. Lean over your round world. Cut off rusty talk with the unfucked woman, the unconvinced friend, the countless uncertain universes, avoid diplomacy with them. Hurry to your appetite. Hurry to your birthright and the night of long knives and grease. Hurry, worker in the realms of song. Hurry angel, covered spirit, minstrel of my greasy pilgrimage. And hurry back to the warm bed where she is sleeping, where it is dark, her face turned away, and you meet in half sleep, kind to each other as if newly met. Sleep against her back, your arm across her dark waist, your hand under her breast. Until she thrashes in her sleep. The flies walk over your face. She does not know how to make you comfortable. She never has. Hurry to sleep. Find a way to get upstairs. The bells have rung, the faithful are breathing frankincense. In a crack of the wood shutters the morning has begun. Hurry to your stretched-out nakedness and to lightly touch yourself as will some time the woman being born. Jiggle your knees, mind worker, hurry through your testament. Invent your song. Invent your power. Hurry to be born in the bed beside her. Hurry to the fish hook. Hurry to your destiny. Hurry to your cunt. Hurry to your vision of G-d. Time is like an arrow. Hurry to the bank. Hurry to your unborn children. Hurry to your thin body and your suntan. Then the slugs will dance, the pure night sky will not mock you. Hurry to your discipline and your bland regime. Move faster than the stain, the fat, the disappointed heart. Hurry to the peanut butter and the cool summer drink. Hurry to your miracle. Hurry to the empty stomach, the victory fast, the unbuilt temple. Wake her up and quarrel in your bed. Eat together through the dark. Seize the round world and stop it from struggling and plant your mouth in the burnt skin. I am your dead voice.

Many thanks for deserting the tongue. Many thanks for the calm breathing of the defeated intelligence. Many thanks for clear intellection in the realms of loss. Many thanks for keeping still while a flood carried off the world. Many thanks for restoring every detail of what it was before.

SLOWLY I MARRIED HER

Slowly I married her
Slowly and bitterly married her love
Married her body
    in her boredom and joy
Slowly I came to her
Slow and resentfully came to her bed
Came to her table
in hunger and habit
    came to be fed
Slowly I married her
sanctioned by none
with nobody's blessings
in nobody's name
    amid general warnings
    amid general scorn
Came to her fragrance
    my nostrils wide
Came to her greed
    with seed for a child
Years in the coming
and years in retreat
    Slowly I married her
Slowly I kneeled
And now we are wounded
    so deep and so well
that no one can hurt us
except Death itself
    And all through Death's dream
I move with her lips

The dream is a night
    but eternal the kiss
And slowly I come to her
    slowly we shed
the clothes of our doubting
    and slowly we wed

received from Nadab and Abihu as they cried with one voice
out of the consuming fire of punishment

received from the king of Ai as he hung from a tree fully
embraced by the reality of his huge mistake

received again and again from the circles of Noah's raven

received from the riot of women in Samson's heart

received from the high forehead of David's giant

and still the heart does not open

received twice from Amnon and Tamar, one pressed on the
other, once in the form of loathing, once in the form of desire

received from Solomon in the strategy of his old age:
the worship of women

received from the first veiled bride whom the bridegroom
did not love

received directly from the honeycomb

received without a language in the Vehicle of Ignorance

and still the heart does not open

received on the crown of my head from the lips of
an eleven-year-old woman in the dark pine fragrance thirty
years ago

received through the crystal of my child's first snowstorm

received from the one who destroyed The Letter of
Consolation, saying: There is no consolation, there is no need
of it

and still the heart does not open

received from the music in my mother's wrist

received from Rosengarten's measuring stick, which is
unmarked like the fretboard of a cello

received from Hershorn as he covers his head and begins to
live without a wife

received from the buttocks of my dark companion as she
dances with my head in the presence of other men
and still the heart does not open
received and received
until we come to the heart that does not need to open
received in six tongues of smoke from the cedar guitar of
the dancer's fiancée
received from the eternal smoke of violins and shoes
and uniforms
received from the extra light of Jesus Christ failing into the
extra world of pain in the new formation: Be your enemy
received from the consecrated ground of a buried pig
received and received
until we come to the heart that is free from opening

END OF MY LIFE IN ART

This is the end of my life in art. At last I have found the woman I was looking for. It is summer. It is the summer I waited for. We are living in a suite on the fifth floor of the Chateau Marmont in Hollywood. She is as beautiful as Lili Marlene. She is as beautiful as Lady Hamilton. Except for the fear of losing her I have no complaint. I have not been denied the full measure of beauty. Nights and mornings we kiss each other. The feathery palms rise through the smog. The curtains stir. The traffic moves on Sunset over painted arrows, words and lines. It is best not even to whisper about this perfection. This is the end of my life in art. I am drinking a Red Needle, a drink I invented in Needles, California, tequila and cranberry juice, lemon and ice. The full measure. I have not been denied the full measure. It happened as I approached my forty-first birthday. Beauty and Love were granted me in the form of a woman. She wears silver bracelets, one on each wrist. I am happy with my luck. Even if she goes away I will say to myself, I have not been denied the full measure of beauty. I said that to myself in Holston, Arizona, in a bar across the street from our motel, when I thought she would be leaving the next morning. This is drunken talk. This is Red Needles talking. It is too smooth. I am frightened. I don't know why. Yesterday I was so frightened that I could hardly hand a Red Needle to a monk on Mt. Baldy. I'm frightened and tired. I am an old man with a silver ornament. These stiff movements should not be accompanied by tiny silver bells. She must be plotting against me in my bed. She wants me to be Carlo Ponti. The black maid is stealing my credit cards. I should go sailing alone through the pine trees. I should get a grip on myself. O god her skin is soft and brown. I would sell my family graves. I am old enough for that. I am old enough to be ruined. I better have another drink. If I could write a song for her I could pay for this suite. She saw the men in Afghanistan, she saw the riders, how can she stay here with me? It is true I am a hero of the Sahara but she did not see me under sand and fire, mastering the sphincters of my cowardice. And she could not know how beautiful these words are. Nobody could. She could not perceive the poignant immortality of my life in art. Nobody can. My vision of the traffic on Sunset Boulevard through the concrete lilies of the balcony railing. The table, the climate, the perfect physique for a forty-year-old artist, famous, happy, frightened. Six in the morning. Six-o-five. The minutes go by. Six-ten. Women. Women and children. The light gone from Los Angeles they say, the original movie light, but this view of Sunset Boulevard satisfactory in every way. My life in art closing down. Monica sleeping. All the wandering mind is hers. My devotions begin to embarrass me. She should grow tired of them soon. I am tired of them now. She is pregnant. Our love-making is sweet because of this. She will not have the child. Six-twenty. We drink Red Needles every night. She tells me of the gay San Francisco world. The weight of her beauty has become intolerable. People in the liquor store actually pop-eyed and double-took as she went by with her long hair and her sacrificial child, her second-hand clothes and her ordinary face mocking all the preparations for allurement here in the heart of Hollywood, so ripe she is in the forces of beauty and music as to frighten me, who has witnessed the end of his life in art. Six-forty. I want to go back to bed and get inside her. That's the only time there's anything approaching peace. And when she sits on my face. When she lowers herself onto my mouth. This feels like doom. This is a pyramid on my chest. I want to change blood with her. I want her slavery. I want her promise. I want her death. I want the thrown acid to disencumber me. I want to stop staring. Six-fifty. Ruined in Los Angeles. I should start smoking again. I'm going to start smoking again. I want to die in her arms and leave her. You need to smoke a pack a day to be that kind of man. When we were on the road I was always ready to drive her to the nearest airport and say goodbye but now I want her to die without me. I started my exercises again today. I need some muscle now. I need a man in the mirror to whisper courage when I shave and to tell me once again about the noble ones who conquered all of this.

HOW TO SPEAK POETRY

Take the word butterfly. To use this word it is not necessary to make the voice weigh less than an ounce or equip it with small dusty wings. It is not necessary to invent a sunny day or a field of daffodils. It is not necessary to be in love, or to be in love with butterflies. The word butterfly is not a real butterfly. There is the word and there is the butterfly. If you confuse these two items people have the right to laugh at you. Do not make so much of the word. Are you trying to suggest that you love butterflies more perfectly than anyone else, or really understand their nature? The word butterfly is merely data. It is not an opportunity for you to hover, soar, befriend flowers, symbolize beauty and frailty, or in any way impersonate a butterfly. Do not act out words. Never act out words. Never try to leave the floor when you talk about flying. Never close your eyes and jerk your head to one side when you talk about death. Do not fix your burning eyes on me when you speak about love. If you want to impress me when you speak about love put your hand in your pocket or under your dress and play with yourself. If ambition and the hunger for applause have driven you to speak about love you should learn how to do it without disgracing yourself or the material.

What is the expression which the age demands? The age demands no expression whatever. We have seen photographs of bereaved Asian mothers. We are not interested in the agony of your fumbled organs. There is nothing you can show on your face that can match the horror of this time. Do not even try. You will only hold yourself up to the scorn of those who have felt things deeply. We have seen newsreels of humans in the extremities of pain and dislocation. Everyone knows you are eating well and are even being paid to stand up there. You are playing to people who have experienced a catastrophe. This should make you very quiet. Speak the words, convey the data, step aside. Everyone knows you are in pain. You cannot tell the audience everything you know about love in every line of love you speak. Step aside and they will know what you know because they know it already. You have nothing to teach them. You are not more beautiful than they are. You are not wiser. Do not shout at them. Do not force a dry entry. That is bad sex. If you show the lines of your genitals, then deliver what you promise. And remember that people do not really want an acrobat in bed. What is our need? To be close to the natural man, to be close to the natural woman. Do not pretend that you are a beloved singer with a vast loyal audience which has followed the ups and downs of your life to this very moment. The bombs, flame-throwers, and all the shit have destroyed more than just the trees and villages. They have also destroyed the stage. Did you think that your profession would escape the general destruction? There is no more stage. There are no more footlights. You are among the people. Then be modest. Speak the words, convey the data, step aside. Be by yourself. Be in your own room. Do not put yourself on.

This is an interior landscape. It is inside. It is private. Respect the privacy of the material. These pieces were written in silence. The courage of the play is to speak them. The discipline of the play is not to violate them. Let the audience feel your love of privacy even though there is no privacy. Be good whores. The poem is not a slogan. It cannot advertise you. It cannot promote your reputation for sensitivity. You are not a stud. You are not a killer lady. All this junk about the gangsters of love. You are students of discipline. Do not act out the words. The words die when you act them out, they wither, and we are left with nothing but your ambition.

Speak the words with the exact precision with which you would check out a laundry list. Do not become emotional about the lace blouse. Do not get a hard-on when you say panties. Do not get all shivery just because of the towel. The sheets should not provoke a dreamy expression about the eyes. There is no need to weep into the handkerchief. The socks are not there to remind you of strange and distant voyages. It is just your laundry. It is just your clothes. Don't peep through them. Just wear them.

The poem is nothing but information. It is the Constitution of the inner country. If you declaim it and blow it up with noble intentions then you are no better than the politicians whom you despise. You are just someone waving a flag and making the cheapest appeal to a kind of emotional patriotism. Think of the words as science, not as art. They are a report. You are speaking before a meeting of the Explorers' Club of the National Geographic Society. These people know all the risks of mountain climbing. They honour you by taking this for granted. If you rub their faces in it that is an insult to their hospitality. Tell them about the height of the mountain, the equipment you used, be specific about the surfaces and the time it took to scale it. Do not work the audience for gasps and sighs. If you are worthy of gasps and sighs it will not be from your appreciation of the event but from theirs. It will be in the statistics and not the trembling of the voice or the cutting of the air with your hands. It will be in the data and the quiet organization of your presence.

Avoid the flourish. Do not be afraid to be weak. Do not be ashamed to be tired. You look good when you're tired. You look like you could go on forever. Now come into my arms. You are the image of my beauty.

I did not want to appear again in these pages except to say goodbye. I thought that he should be left alone in this most delicate phase of the wedding preparation, with the man asleep and the woman being born. I thought he could be trusted to maintain the balance. He can't. It is too quiet for him. He has to shoot off his fucking Sunday School mouth. We're supposed to sit back and listen to The Good Guy talking, the old crapulous Dogma of Decency. This filth cannot go unpunished. How dare he summon the widows of Asia to his side! How dare he break his vow of silence to lecture, in the name of The People, from the shit-stained marble balcony of his obscene cultural delusions! I hate him for this. He will pay for this religious advertisement. He will carry the syrup of it in his balls. He will pass this life as a teddy bear. Death to the Commissars of the Left and the Right! Death to the Commissars of Mystery! I hate his fucking face, all serious with concern. Don't let him into the good movie, and don't let him hear any of the merry tunes in the Music Hall. Never let him sing again. And let him sit outside with his stinking educational corpse while the stripper on the little gilded stage turns every one of us on.

THE POLITICS OF THIS BOOK

Years ago I sat in this garden, at this very table, among the ancestors of yellow daisies that surround me now. I was drugged and happy then. I wrote deep from my sunstroke. Enough of the past. It is a morning in March 1975.

The bumblebees have arrived. There are noisy birds in the rain gutter. One thread of a spider web, suddenly white, goes fishing in the sunshine. Some butterflies want to fertilize my shiny boot. A cat sharpens the top of a wall by walking across it, and then by walking back, adjusts the horizontal.

I won't be sitting here long. I'm in a terrible hurry. I'm going to Jerusalem. I'm going with the happy Israeli soldiers and I'm going with the King of Saudi Arabia to kneel down in the place that we were promised.

A bee enters a hanging yellow flower like a woman pulling a gown over her head, shivering, struggling upwards. The sun climbs to the middle of the sky and stops. It's noon. The bells of noon ringing loud from the cathedral tower. Great shovelfuls of sound dumped into the grave of our activity. The sound fills up every space and every thought. The past is plugged up. Layer after layer of the present seizes us, buries us in one vast amber paperweight.

I won't be going to Jerusalem after all. You will have to go to Jerusalem alone. It is yours. It was given to you by the angels of culture and time. But I can't go. And I can't loosen your interest in the war. You will want to "challenge the sphincters of your cowardice under sand and fire." Goodbye.

I will be here if you look back, at this very table, in this very garden where the bumblebee charges like a bull into the yellow trumpet, and the sun makes a dent in my black trousers, and my wife repeats on a loop "Did you smell the ambrosia of the universe in my little cunt?" and the birds tune up at last.

YOU'RE NOT SUPPOSED
TO BE HERE

You're not supposed to be here
Not supposed to be looking for me
This is the poor side of silence
This is the white noise
          of the abandoned appliance
This is The Captivity

You need details
You need the name of a street
You're not supposed to be here
          in the Name of G-d

You're waiting for me again
Waiting at the mouth
          of the Tunnel of Love
But where is the cold little river
Where is the painted boat

If only the hummingbird
would sip at your desire
If only the green leaves
could use your longing
If only a woman were looking
over your shoulder
at a map of the Eternal city

It seems that nothing can take you away
from this odd memorial
Nothing that's been made or born
separate you from
          the fiction of my absence

All the Messiahs are with me in this
You're not supposed to be here
All the Messiahs agree
You're not supposed to be looking for me

FINAL EXAMINATION

I am almost 90
Everyone I know has died off
except Leonard
He can still be seen
hobbling with his love

COMMENTARY — FINAL EXAMINATION

I have examined his death. Although it is unstable, I doubt that we shall find the old goat nibbling again at the lacy hem of the various salvations. I am more vulgar than he was, but I never pretended to a spiritual exercise. Furthermore, his death is sexless and cannot be used in politics. There is a cheap sweet smell in the air for which he bears some responsibility. I swear to the police that I have appeared, and do appear, as one of his voices. I see in the insignificance of these pages a shadow of the coming modesty. His death belongs to the future. I am well read. I am well served. I am satisfied and I give in. Long live the marriage of men and women. Long live the one heart.

RECENT SONGS

CAME SO FAR FOR BEAUTY

I came so far for beauty
I left so much behind:
my patience and my family,
my masterpiece unsigned

I thought I'd be rewarded
for such a very lonely choice,
and surely she would answer
to such a hopeless voice

I practised on my sainthood
I gave to one and all
but the rumours of my virtue
they moved her not at all

I changed my style to silver
I changed my clothes to black
and where I did surrender,
now I would attack

I stormed the old casino
for the money and the flesh,
and I myself decided
what was rotten, what was fresh

And men to do my bidding
and broken bones to teach
the value of my pardon
the shadow of my reach

But no I could not touch her
with such a heavy hand;
her star beyond my order,
her nakedness unmanned

I came so far for beauty
I left so much behind:
my patience and my family,
my masterpiece unsigned

THE WINDOW

Why do you stand by the window
abandoned to beauty and pride?
the thorn of the night in your bosom,
the spear of the age in your side;
lost in the rages of fragrance,
lost in the rags of remorse,
lost in the waves of a sickness
that loosens the high silver nerves.

O chosen love, O frozen love
O tangle of matter and ghost.
O darling of angels, demons and saints
and the whole broken-hearted host —
    Gentle this soul.

Come forth from the cloud of unknowing
and kiss the cheek of the moon;
the code of solitude broken,
why tarry confused and alone?
And leave no word of discomfort,
and leave no observer to mourn,
but climb on your tears and be silent
like the rose on its ladder of thorn.

Then lay your rose on the fire;
the fire give up to the sun;
the sun give over to splendour
in the arms of the High Holy One;
for the Holy One dreams of a letter,
dreams of a letter's death —
oh bless the continuous stutter
of the word being made into flesh.

O chosen love, O frozen love
O tangle of matter and ghost.
O darling of angels, demons and saints
and the whole broken-hearted host —
    Gentle this soul,
    gentle this soul.

OUR LADY OF SOLITUDE

All summer long she touched me
She gathered in my soul
From many a thorn, from many a thicket
Her fingers like a weaver's, quick and cool

And the light came from her body
And the night went through her grace
All summer long she touched me
And I knew her, I knew her face to face

And her dress was blue and silver
And her words were few and small
She is the vessel of the whole wide world
Mistress, oh mistress of us all

Dear Lady, Queen of Solitude
I thank you with my heart
For keeping me so close to thee
While so many, oh so many stood apart

And the light came from her body
And the night went through her grace
All summer long she touched me
And I knew her, I knew her face to face

THE GYPSY WIFE

Where where where
is my gypsy wife tonight?
I've heard all the wild reports;
they can't be right.
But whose head is this she's dancing with
on the threshing floor?
Whose darkness deepens in her arms
a little more?
And where
where is my gypsy wife tonight?

The silver knives are flashing
in the tired old café.
A ghost climbs on the table
in a bridal negligee.
She says, "My body is the light,
my body is the way."
I raise my arm against it all
and I catch the bride's bouquet.
And where
where is my gypsy wife tonight?

Too early for the rainbow,
too early for the dove.
These are the final days:
this is the darkness, this is the flood.
And there is no man or woman
who can be touched,
but you who come between them,
you will be judged.

And where
where is my gypsy wife tonight,
where where where
is my gypsy wife tonight?

THE TRAITOR

Now the swan it floated on the English River;
the rose of high romance it opened wide;
a suntanned woman yawned me through the summer;
the judges watched us from the other side.

I told my mother, "Mother, I must leave you.
Preserve my room, but not shed a tear.
Should rumours of a shabby ending reach you,
it was half my fault and half the atmosphere."

But the rose I sickened with a scarlet fever
and the swan I tempted with a sense of shame;
she said at last I was her finest lover,
and if she withered I would be to blame.

The judges said, "You missed it by a fraction.
Rise up and brace your troops for the attack.
The dreamers ride against the men of action,
oh see the men of action falling back."

But I lingered on her thighs a fatal moment,
I kissed her lips as though I thirsted still.
My falsity, it stung me like a hornet;
the poison sank and it paralyzed my will.

I could not move to warn all the younger soldiers
that they had been deserted from above;
so on battlefields from here to Barcelona
I'm listed with the enemies of love.

And long ago she said, "I must be leaving,
but keep my body here to lie upon.
You can move it up and down, and when I'm sleeping,
run some wire through that rose and wind the swan."

So daily I renew my idle duty;
I touch her here and there, I know my place;
I kiss her open mouth, I praise her beauty,
and people call me traitor to my face.

THE GUESTS

One by one the guests arrive
The guests are coming through
The open-hearted many
The broken-hearted few

And no one knows where the night is going
And no one knows why the wine is flowing
O love, I need you, I need you, I need you
I need you now

And those who dance begin to dance
And those who weep begin
Welcome, welcome, cries a voice
Let all my guests come in

And all go stumbling through that house
In lonely secrecy
Saying, *Do reveal yourself*
Or, *Why hast thou forsaken me*

All at once the torches flare
The inner door flies open
One by one they enter there
In every style of passion

And here they take their sweet repast
While house and grounds dissolve
And one by one the guests are cast
beyond the garden walls

And those who dance begin to dance
Those who weep begin
And those who earnestly are lost
Are lost and lost again

One by one the guests arrive
The guests are coming through
The broken-hearted many
The open-hearted few

And no one knows where the night is going
And no one knows why the wine is flowing
O love, I need you, I need you, I need you
I need you now

BALLAD OF THE ABSENT MARE

Say a prayer for the cowboy, his mare's run away
and he'll walk till he finds her, his darling, his stray
But the river's in flood and the roads are awash
and the bridges break up in the panic of loss

And there's nothing to follow, there's nowhere to go
She's gone like the summer, she's gone like the snow
And the crickets are breaking his heart with their song
as the day caves in and the night is all wrong

Did he dream, was it she who went galloping past
and bent down the fern and broke open the grass
and printed the mud with the iron and the gold
that he nailed to her feet when he was the lord

And though she goes grazing a minute away
he tracks her all night and he tracks her all day;
blind to her presence except to compare
his injury here with her punishment there

Then at home on his branch in the highest tree
a songbird sings out so suddenly
Oh the sun is warm and the soft winds ride
on the willow trees by the riverside

And the world is sweet and the world is wide
and she's there where the light and the darkness divide
and the steam's coming off her, she's huge and she's shy
and she steps on the moon when she paws at the sky

And she comes to his hand but she's not really tame
She longs to be lost and he longs for the same
And she'll bolt and she'll plunge through the first open pass
to roll and to feed in the sweet mountain grass

Or she'll make a break for the high plateau
where there's nothing above and there's nothing below
And it's time for their burden, it's time for the whip
Will she walk through the flame, can he shoot from the hip

So he binds himself to the galloping mare
and she binds herself to the rider there
and there is no space but there's left and right
and there is no time but there's day and night

And he leans on her neck and he whispers low
Whither thou goest I will go
And they turn as one and they head for the plain
no need for the whip, no need for the rein

Now the clasp of this union, who fastens it tight
who snaps it asunder the very next night?
Some say the rider, some say the mare
some say love's like the smoke, beyond all repair

But my darling says, Leonard, just let it go by,
that old silhouette on the great Western sky
So I pick out a tune and they move right along
and they're gone like the smoke, they're gone like this song

BOOK OF MERCY

I stopped to listen, but he did not come. I began again with a sense of loss. As this sense deepened I heard him again. I stopped stopping and I stopped starting, and I allowed myself to be crushed by ignorance. This was a strategy, and didn't work at all. Much time, years were wasted in such a minor mode. I bargain now. I offer buttons for his love. I beg for mercy. Slowly he yields. Haltingly he moves toward his throne. Reluctantly the angels grant to one another permission to sing. In a transition so delicate it cannot be marked, the court is established on beams of golden symmetry, and once again I am a singer in the lower choirs, born fifty years ago to raise my voice this high, and no higher.

When I left the king began to rehearse what I would say to the world: long rehearsals full of revisions, imaginary applause, humiliations, edicts of revenge. I grew swollen as I conspired with my ambition, I struggled, I expanded, and when the term was up, I gave birth to an ape. After some small inevitable misunderstanding, the ape turned on me. Limping, stumbling, I fled back to the swept courtyards of the king. "Where is your ape?" the king demanded. "Bring me your ape." The work is slow. The ape is old. He clowns behind his bars, imitating our hands in the dream. He winks at my official sense of urgency. What king? he wants to know. What courtyard? What highway?

I HEARD MY SOUL SINGING

I heard my soul singing behind a leaf, plucked the leaf, but then I heard it singing behind a veil. I tore the veil, but then I heard it singing behind a wall. I broke the wall, and I heard my soul singing against me. I built up the wall, mended the curtain, but I could not put back the leaf. I held it in my hand and I heard my soul singing mightily against me. This is what it's like to study without a friend.

SIT DOWN, MASTER

Sit down, master, on this rude chair of praises, and rule my nervous heart with your great decrees of freedom. Out of time you have taken me to do my daily task. Out of mist and dust you have fashioned me to know the numberless worlds between the crown and the kingdom. In utter defeat I came to you and you received me with a sweetness I had not dared to remember. Tonight I come to you again, soiled by strategies and trapped in the loneliness of my tiny domain. Establish your law in this walled place. Let nine men come to lift me into their prayer so that I may whisper with them: Blessed be the name of the glory of the kingdom forever and forever.

IN THE EYES OF MEN

In the eyes of men he falls, and in his own eyes too. He falls from his high place, he trips on his achievement. He falls to you, he falls to know you. It is sad, they say. See his disgrace, say the ones at his heel. But he falls radiantly toward the light to which he falls. They cannot see who lifts him as he falls, or how his falling changes, and he himself bewildered till his heart cries out to bless the one who holds him in his falling. And in his fall he hears his heart cry out, his heart explains why he is falling, why he had to fall, and he gives over to the fall. Blessed are you, clasp of the falling. He falls into the sky, he falls into the light, none can hurt him as he falls. Blessed are you, shield of the falling. Wrapped in his fall, concealed within his fall, he finds the place, he is gathered in. While his hair streams back and his clothes tear in the wind, he is held up, comforted, he enters into the place of his fall. Blessed are you, embrace of the falling, foundation of the light, master of the human accident.

BLESSED ARE YOU

Blessed are you who has given each man a shield of loneliness so that he cannot forget you. You are the truth of loneliness, and only your name addresses it. Strengthen my loneliness that I may be healed in your name, which is beyond all consolations that are uttered on this earth. Only in your name can I stand in the rush of time, only when this loneliness is yours can I lift my sins toward your mercy.

YOU HAVE SWEETENED YOUR WORD

You have sweetened your word on my lips. My son too has heard the song that does not belong to him. From Abraham to Augustine, the nations have not known you, though every cry, every curse is raised on the foundation of your holiness. You placed me in this mystery and you let me sing, though only from this curious corner. You bound me to my fingerprints, as you bind every man, except the ones who need no binding. You led me to this field where I can dance with a broken knee. You led me safely to this night, you gave me a crown of darkness and light, and tears to greet my enemy. Who can tell of your glory, who can number your forms, who dares expound the interior life of G-d? And now you feed my household, you gather them to sleep, to dream, to dream freely, you surround them with the fence of all that I have seen. Sleep, my son, my small daughter, sleep — this night, this mercy has no boundaries.

I DRAW ASIDE THE CURTAIN

I draw aside the curtain. You mock us with the beauty of your world. My heart hates the trees, the wind moving the branches, the dead diamond machinery of the sky. I pace the corridor between my teeth and my bladder, angry, murderous, comforted by the smell of my sweat. I weakened myself in your name. In my own eyes I disgraced myself for trusting you, against all evidence, against the prevailing winds of horror, over the bully's laughter, the torturer's loyalty, the sweet questions of the sly. Find me here, you whom David found in hell. The skeletons are waiting for your famous mechanical salvation. Swim through the blood, father of mercy. Broadcast your light through the apple of pain, radiant one, sourceless, source of light. I wait for you, king of the dead, here in this garden where you placed me, beside the poisonous grass, miasmal homesteads, black Hebrew gibberish of pruned grapevines. I wait for you in the springtime of beatings and gross unnecessary death. Direct me out of this, O magnet of the falling cherry petals. Make a truce between my disgust and the impeccable landscape of fields and milky towns. Crush my swollen smallness, infiltrate my shame. Broken in the unemployment of my soul, I have driven a wedge into your world, fallen on both sides of it. Count me back to your mercy with the measures of a bitter song, and do not separate me from my tears.

FRIEND, WHEN YOU SPEAK

Friend, when you speak this carefully I know it is because you don't know what to say. I listen in such a way so as not to add to your confusion. I make some reply at every opportunity so as not to compound your loneliness. Thus the conversation continues under an umbrella of optimism. If you suggest a feeling, I affirm it. If you provoke, I accept the challenge. The surface is thick, but it has its flaws, and hopefully we will trip on one of them. Now, we can order a meat sandwich for the protein, or we can take our places in the Sanhedrin and determine what it is to be done with those great cubes of diamond that our teacher Moses shouldered down the mountain. You want to place them in such a way that the sun by day, and the moon and stars by night, will shine through them. I suggest another perspective which would include the light of the celestial bodies within the supernal radiance of the cubes. We lean toward each other over the table. The dust mingles with the mist, our nostrils widen. We are definitely interested; now we can get down to a Jew's business.

MY TEACHER

My teacher gave me what I do not need, told me what I need not know. At a high price he sold me water beside the river. In the middle of a dream he led me gently to my bed. He threw me out when I was crawling, took me in when I was home. He referred me to the crickets when I had to sing, and when I tried to be alone he fastened me to a congregation. He curled his fists and pounded me toward my proper shape. He puked in disgust when I swelled without filling. He sank his tiger teeth into everything of mine that I refused to claim. He drove me through the pine trees at an incredible speed to that realm where I barked with a dog, slid with the shadows, and leaped from a point of view. He let me be a student of a love that I will never be able to give. He suffered me to play at friendship with my truest friend. When he was certain that I was incapable of self-reform, he flung me across the fence of the Torah.

ISRAEL

Israel, and you who call yourself Israel, the Church that calls itself Israel, and the revolt that calls itself Israel, and every nation chosen to be a nation — none of these lands is yours, all of you are thieves of holiness, all of you at war with Mercy. Who will say it? Will America say, We have stolen it, or France step down? Will Russia confess, or Poland say, We have sinned? All bloated on their scraps of destiny, all swaggering in the immunity of superstition. Ishmael, who was saved in the wilderness, and given shade in the desert, and a deadly treasure under you: has Mercy made you wise? Will Ishmael declare, We are in debt forever? Therefore the lands belong to none of you, the borders do not hold, the Law will never serve the lawless. To every people the land is given on condition. Perceived or not, there is a Covenant, beyond the constitution, beyond sovereign guarantee, beyond the nation's sweetest dreams of itself. The Covenant is broken, the condition is dishonoured, have you not noticed that the world has been taken away? You have no place, you will wander through yourselves from generation to generation without a thread. Therefore you rule over chaos, you hoist your flags with no authority, and the heart that is still alive hates you, and the remnant of Mercy is ashamed to look at you. You decompose behind your flimsy armour, your stench alarms you, your panic strikes at love. The land is not yours, the land has been taken back, your shrines fall through empty air, your tablets are quickly revised, and you bow down in hell beside your hired torturers, and still you count your battalions and crank out your marching songs. Your righteous enemy is listening. He hears your anthems full of blood and vanity, and your children singing to themselves. He has overturned the vehicle of nationhood, he has spilled the precious cargo, and every nation he has taken back. Because you are swollen with your little time. Because you do not wrestle with your angel. Because you dare to live without G-d. Because your cowardice has led you to believe that the victor does not limp.

YOU WHO POUR MERCY INTO HELL

You who pour mercy into hell, sole authority in the highest and the lowest worlds, let your anger disperse the mist in this aimless place, where even my sins fall short of the mark. Let me be with you again, absolute companion, let me study your ways which are just beyond the hope of evil. Seize my heart out of its fantasy, direct my heart from the fiction of secrecy, you who know the secrets of every heart, whose mercy is to be the secret of longing. Let every heart declare its secret, let every song disclose your love, let us bring to you the sorrows of our freedom. Blessed are you, who opens a gate, in every moment, to enter in truth or tarry in hell. Let me be with you again, let me put this away, you who wait beside me, who have broken down your world to gather hearts. Blessed is your name, blessed is the confession of your name. Kindle the darkness of my calling, let me cry to the one who judges the heart in justice and mercy. Arouse my heart again with the limitless breath you breathe into me, arouse the secret from obscurity.

WHEN I HAVE NOT RAGE

When I have not rage or sorrow, and you depart from me, then I am most afraid. When the belly is full, and the mind has its sayings, then I fear for my soul; I rush to you as a child at night breaks into its parents' room. Do not forget me in my satisfaction. When the heart grins at itself, the world is destroyed. And I am found alone with the husks and the shells. Then the dangerous moment comes: I am too great to ask for help. I have other hopes. I legislate from the fortress of my disappointments, with a set jaw. Overthrow this even terror with a sweet remembrance: when I was with you, when my soul delighted you, when I was what you wanted. My heart sings of your longing for me, and my thoughts climb down to marvel at your mercy. I do not fear as you gather up my days. Your name is the sweetness of time, and you carry me close into the night, speaking consolations, drawing down lights from the sky, saying, See how the night has no terror for one who remembers the Name.

WE CRY OUT

We cry out for what we have lost, and we remember you again. We look for each other, we cannot find us, and we remember you. From the ground of no purpose our children accuse us, and we remember, we recall a purpose. Could it be? we wonder. And here is death. Could it possibly be? And here is old age. And we never knew; we never stood up, and the good land was taken from us, and the sweet family was crushed. Maybe, we said, it could be, and we gave it a place among the possibilities. I'll do it myself, we said, as shame thickened the faculties of the heart. And the first reports were of failure, and the second of mutilations, and the third of every abomination. We remember, we cry out to you to return our soul. Is it really upon us? Yes, it is upon us. Do we merit this? Yes, we merit this. We cry out for what we have lost, and we remember you. We remember the containing word, the holy channels of commandment, and goodness waiting forever on the Path. And here and there, among the seventy tongues and the hundred darknesses — something, something shining, men of courage strengthening themselves to kindle the lights of repentance.

You who question souls, and you to whom souls must answer, do not cut off the soul of my son on my account. Let the strength of his childhood lead him to you, and the joy of his body stand him upright in your eyes. May he discern my prayer for him, and to whom it is uttered, and in what shame. I received the living waters and I held them in a stagnant pool. I was taught but I did not teach. I was loved but I did not love. I weakened the name that spoke me, and I chased the light with my own understanding. Whisper in his ear. Direct him to a place of learning. Illuminate his child's belief in mightiness. Rescue him from those who want him with no soul, who have their channels in the bedrooms of the rich and poor, to draw the children into death. Let him see me coming back. Allow us to bring forth our souls together to make a place for your name. If I am too late, redeem my yearning in his heart, bless him with a soul that remembers you, that he may uncover it with careful husbandry. They who wish to devour him have grown powerful on my idleness. They have a number for him, and a chain. Let him see them withered in the light of your name. Let him see their dead kingdom from the mountain of your word. Stand him up upon his soul, bless him with the truth of manhood.

IT IS ALL AROUND ME

It is all around me, the darkness. You are my only shield. Your name is my only light. What love I have, your law is the source, this dead love that remembers only its name, yet the name is enough to open itself like a mouth, to call down the dew, and drink. O dead name that through your mercy speaks to the living name, mercy harkening to the will that is bent toward it, the will whose strength is its pledge to you — O name of love, draw down the blessings of completion on the man you have cut in half to know you.

IT IS TO YOU I TURN

It is to you I turn. The table stands on tiptoe. Every object leaps to its place. The closed book rises on its thousand pages and my wakefulness rejoices. I turn to you, my song in the house of night, my shield against the quarrels. I turn to you, who unifies the upward heart. Your name is the foundation of the night. The Accuser, with his thousand voices, stands in the place you are not named. Blessed is the name that holds this house in the firmness of mercy, and binds this song to the rock.

HOLY IS YOUR NAME

Holy is your name, holy is your work, holy are the days that return to you. Holy are the years that you uncover. Holy are the hands that are raised to you, and the weeping that is wept to you. Holy is the fire between your will and ours, in which we are refined. Holy is that which is unredeemed, covered with your patience. Holy are the souls lost in your unnaming. Holy, and shining with a great light, is every living thing, established in this world and covered with time, until your name is praised forever.

NOT KNOWING WHERE TO GO

Not knowing where to go, I go to you. Not knowing where to turn, I turn to you. Not knowing what to hold, I bind myself to you. Having lost my way, I make my way to you. Having soiled my heart, I lift my heart to you. Having wasted my days, I bring the heap to you. The great highway covered with debris, I travel on a hair to you. The wall smeared with filth, I go through a pinhole of light. Blocked by every thought, I fly on the wisp of a remembrance. Defeated by silence. here is a place where the silence is more subtle. And here is the opening in defeat. And here is the clasp of the will. And here is the fear of you. And here is the fastening of mercy. Blessed are you, in this man's moment. Blessed are you, whose presence illuminates outrageous evil. Blessed are you who brings chains out of the darkness. Blessed are you, who waits in the world. Blessed are you, whose name is in the world.

ALL MY LIFE

All my life is broken unto you, and all my glory soiled unto you. Do not let the spark of my soul go out in the even sadness. Let me raise the brokenness to you, to the world where the breaking is for love. Do not let the words be mine, but change them into truth. With these lips instruct my heart, and let fall into the world what is broken in the world. Lift me up to the wrestling of faith. Do not leave me where the sparks go out, and the jokes are told in the dark, and new things are called forth and appraised in the scale of the terror. Face me to the rays of love, O source of light, or face me to the majesty of your darkness, but not here, do not leave me here, where death is forgotten, and the new thing grins.

I LOST MY WAY

I lost my way, I forgot to call on your name. The raw heart beat against the world, and the tears were for my lost victory. But you are here. You have always been here. The world is all forgetting, and the heart is a rage of directions, but your name unifies the heart, and the world is lifted into its place. Blessed is the one who waits in the traveller's heart for his turning.

VARIOUS POSITIONS

DANCE ME TO THE END OF LOVE

Dance me to your beauty
with a burning violin
Dance me through the panic
till I'm gathered safely in
Lift me like an olive branch
and be my homeward dove
Dance me to the end of love

Let me see your beauty
when the witnesses are gone
Let me feel you moving
like they do in Babylon
Show me slowly what I only
know the limits of
Dance me to the end of love

Dance me to the wedding now
dance me on and on
Dance me very tenderly and
dance me very long
We're both of us beneath our love
we're both of us above
Dance me to the end of love

Dance me to the children
who are asking to be born
Dance me through the curtains
that our kisses have outworn
Raise a tent of shelter now
though every thread is torn
Dance me to the end of love

Dance me to your beauty
with a burning violin
Dance me through the panic
till I'm gathered safely in
Touch me with your naked hand
touch me with your glove
Dance me to the end of love

COMING BACK TO YOU

Maybe I'm still hurting,
I can't turn the other cheek.
But you know that I still love you;
it's just that I can't speak.
I looked for you in everyone
and they called me on that too;
I lived alone but I was only
coming back to you

They're shutting down the factory now
just when all the bills are due;
and the fields they're under lock and key
though the rain and the sun come through.
And springtime starts but then it stops
in the name of something new;
and all my senses rise against this
coming back to you

They're handing down my sentence now,
and I know what I must do:
another mile of silence while I'm
coming back to you

There are many in your life
and many still to be.
Since you are a shining light,
there's many that you'll see.
But I have to deal with envy
when you choose the precious few
who've left their pride on the other side of
coming back to you

Even in your arms I know
I'll never get it right;
even when you bend
to give me comfort in the night.
I've got to have your word on this
or none of it is true,
and all I've said was just instead of
coming back to you

THE CAPTAIN

The Captain called me to his bed
he fumbled for my hand.
"Take these silver bars," he said,
"I'm giving you command."

"Command of what? there's no one here,
there's only you and me —
All the rest are dead or in retreat
or with the enemy."

"Complain, complain, that's all you've done
ever since we lost.
If it's not the Crucifixion
then it's the Holocaust."

"May Christ have mercy on your soul
for making such a joke
amid these hearts that burned like coal
and flesh that rose like smoke."

"I know that you have suffered, lad,
but suffer this a while:
Whatever makes a soldier sad
will make a killer smile."

"I'm leaving, Captain, I must go;
there's blood upon your hand.
But tell me, Captain, if you know
of a decent place to stand."

"There is no decent place to stand
in a massacre,
but if a woman take your hand,
then go and stand with her."

"I left a wife in Tennessee
and a baby in Saigon —
I risked my life, but not to hear
some country-western song."

"But if you cannot raise your love
to a very high degree,
then you're just the man I'm thinking of —
so come and stand with me."

"Your standing days are done," I cried,
"you'll rally me no more.
I don't even know what side
we fought on, or what for."

"I'm on the side that's always lost
against the side of heaven;
I'm on the side of snake-eyes tossed
against the side of seven.

"And I've read the Bill of Human Rights
and some of it was true,
but there wasn't any burden left
so I'm laying one on you."

Now the Captain he was dying
but the Captain wasn't hurt.
The silver bars were in my hand;
I pinned them to my shirt.

IF IT BE YOUR WILL

If it be your will
that I speak no more,
and my voice be still
as it was before;
I will speak no more,
I shall abide until
I am spoken for,
if it be your will.

If it be your will
that a voice be true,
from this broken hill
I will sing to you.
From this broken hill
all your praises they shall ring
if it be your will
to let me sing.

If it be your will,
if there is a choice,
let the rivers fill,
let the hills rejoice.
Let your mercy spill
on all these burning hearts in hell,
if it be your will
to make us well.

And draw us near
and bind us tight,
all your children here
in their rags of light;
in our rags of light,
all dressed to kill;
and end this night,
if it be your will.

THE NIGHT COMES ON

I went down to the place where I knew she lay waiting
under the marble and the snow.
I said, "Mother, I'm frightened; the thunder and the lightning;
I'll never come through this alone."
She said, *"I'll be with you, my shawl wrapped around you,
my hand on your head when you go."*
And the night came on; it was very calm;
I wanted the night to go on and on,
but she said, *"Go back, go back to the world."*

We were fighting in Egypt, when they signed this agreement
that nobody else had to die.
There was this terrible sound and my father went down
with a terrible wound in his side.
He said, *"Try to go on, take my books, take my gun,
and remember, my son, how they lied."*
And the night comes on, and it's very calm;
I'd like to pretend that my father was wrong,
but you don't want to lie, not to the young.

We were locked in this kitchen; I took to religion,
and I wondered how long she would stay.
I needed so much to have nothing to touch:
I've always been greedy that way.
But my son and my daughter climbed out of the water,
crying, *"Papa, you promised to play."*
And they lead me away to the great surprise;
it's *"Papa, don't peek, Papa, cover your eyes."*
And they hide, they hide in the world.

Now I look for her always; I'm lost in this calling;
I'm tied to the threads of some prayer.
Saying, "When will she summon me, when will she come to me,
what must I do to prepare?" —
Then she bends to my longing, like a willow, like a fountain,
she stands in the luminous air.
And the night comes on, and it's very calm,
I lie in her arms, she says, *"When I'm gone*
I'll be yours, yours for a song."

The crickets are singing, the vesper bells ringing,
the cat's curled asleep in his chair.
I'll go down to Bill's Bar, I can make it that far,
and I'll see if my friends are still there.
Yes, and here's to the few who forgive what you do,
and the fewer who don't even care!
And the night comes on; it's very calm;
I want to cross over, I want to go home,
but she says, *"Go back, go back to the world."*

HALLELUJAH

I've heard there was a secret chord
that David played to please the Lord,
but you don't really care for music, do you?
It goes like this: the fourth, the fifth
the minor fall, the major lift;
the baffled king composing Hallelujah!

Your faith was strong but you needed proof.
You saw her bathing on the roof;
her beauty and the moonlight overthrew you.
She tied you to a kitchen chair
she broke your throne, she cut your hair,
and from your lips she drew the Hallelujah!

You say I took the Name in vain;
I don't even know the name.
But if I did, well, really, what's it to you?
There's a blaze of light in every word;
it doesn't matter which you heard,
the holy, or the broken Hallelujah!

I did my best; it wasn't much.
I couldn't feel, so I learned to touch.
I've told the truth, I didn't come to fool you.
And even though it all went wrong,
I'll stand before the Lord of Song
with nothing on my lips but Hallelujah!

(Additional verses)

Baby, I've been here before.
I know this room, I've walked this floor.
I used to live alone before I knew you.
I've seen your flag on the marble arch,
but love is not a victory march,
it's a cold and it's a broken Hallelujah!

There was a time you let me know
what's really going on below
but now you never show it to me, do you?
I remember when I moved in you,
and the holy dove was moving too,
and every breath we drew was Hallelujah!

Now maybe there's a God above
but all I ever learned from love
is how to shoot at someone who outdrew you.
And it's no complaint you hear tonight,
and it's not some pilgrim who's seen the light —
it's a cold and it's a broken Hallelujah!

I'M YOUR MAN

FIRST WE TAKE MANHATTAN

They sentenced me to twenty years of boredom for trying to change the system from within. I'm coming now, I'm coming to reward them. First we take Manhattan, then we take Berlin.

I'm guided by a signal in the heavens. I'm guided by the birthmark on my skin. I'm guided by the beauty of our weapons. First we take Manhattan, then we take Berlin.

I'd really like to live beside you, baby. I love your body and your spirit and your clothes. But you see that line that's moving through the station? I told you, I told you, I told you that I was one of those.

You loved me as a loser, but now you're worried that I just might win. You know the way to stop me, but you don't have the discipline. How many nights I prayed for this, to let my work begin. First we take Manhattan, then we take Berlin.

I don't like your fashion business, mister. I don't like these drugs that keep you thin. I don't like what happened to my sister. First we take Manhattan, then we take Berlin.

I'd really like to live beside you, baby. I love your body and your spirit and your clothes. But you see that line that's moving through the station? I told you, I told you, I told you that I was one of those.

And I thank you for the items that you sent me: the monkey and the plywood violin. I've practised every night and now I'm ready. First we take Manhattan, then we take Berlin.

Remember me? I used to live for music. Remember me? I brought your groceries in. It's Father's Day, and everybody's wounded. First we take Manhattan, then we take Berlin.

TAKE THIS WALTZ

(After Lorca)

Now in Vienna there are ten pretty women.
There's a shoulder where death comes to cry.
There's a lobby with nine hundred windows.
There's a tree where the doves go to die.
There's a piece that was torn from the morning,
and it hangs in the Gallery of Frost —
Ay, ay ay ay
Take this waltz, take this waltz,
take this waltz with the clamp on its jaws.

I want you, I want you, I want you
on a chair with a dead magazine.
In the cave at the tip of the lily,
in some hallway where love's never been.
On a bed where the moon has been sweating,
in a cry filled with footsteps and sand —
Ay, ay ay ay
Take this waltz, take this waltz,
take its broken waist in your hand.

This waltz, this waltz, this waltz, this waltz
with its very own breath
of brandy and death,
dragging its tail in the sea.

There's a concert hall in Vienna
where your mouth had a thousand reviews.
There's a bar where the boys have stopped talking,
they've been sentenced to death by the blues.
Ah, but who is it climbs to your picture
with a garland of freshly cut tears?
Ay, ay ay ay
Take this waltz, take this waltz,
take this waltz, it's been dying for years.

There's an attic where children are playing,
where I've got to lie down with you soon,
in a dream of Hungarian lanterns,
in the mist of some sweet afternoon.
And I'll see what you've chained to your sorrow,
all your sheep and your lilies of snow —
Ay, ay ay ay
Take this waltz, take this waltz
with its "I'll never forget you, you know!"

And I'll dance with you in Vienna,
I'll be wearing a river's disguise.
The hyacinth wild on my shoulder
my mouth on the dew of your thighs.
And I'll bury my soul in a scrapbook,
with the photographs there and the moss.
And I'll yield to the flood of your beauty,
my cheap violin and my cross.
And you'll carry me down on your dancing
to the pools that you lift on your wrist —
O my love, o my love
Take this waltz, take this waltz,
it's yours now. It's all that there is.

AIN'T NO CURE FOR LOVE

I loved you for a long long time. I know this love is real. It don't matter how it all went wrong. That don't change the way I feel. And I can't believe that time can heal this wound I'm speaking of — *There ain't no cure, there ain't no cure, there ain't no cure for love.*

I'm aching for you, baby. I can't pretend I'm not. I need to see you naked in your body and your thought. I've got you like a habit and I'll never get enough — *There ain't no cure, there ain't no cure, there ain't no cure for love.*

All the rocket ships are climbing through the sky, the holy books are open wide, the doctors working day and night, but they'll never ever find that cure for love — there ain't no drink, no drug — there's nothing pure enough to be a cure for love.

I see you in the subway and I see you on the bus. I see you lying down with me and I see you waking up. I see your hand, I see your hair, your bracelets and your brush. And I call to you, I call to you, but I don't call soft enough — *There ain't no cure, there ain't no cure, there ain't no cure for love.*

I walked into this empty church — I had no place else to go — when the sweetest voice I ever heard came whispering to my soul. I don't need to be forgiven for loving you so much. It's written in the scriptures, it's written there in blood. I even heard the angels declare it from above — *There ain't no cure, there ain't no cure, there ain't no cure for love.*

I'M YOUR MAN

If you want a lover
I'll do anything you ask me to
If you want another kind of love
I'll wear a mask for you
If you want a partner
take my hand, or
if you want to strike me
down in anger
here I stand
    I'm your man

If you want a boxer
I will step into the ring for you
If you want a doctor
I'll examine every inch of you
If you want a driver
climb inside
or if you want to take me
for a ride
you know you can
    I'm your man

The moon's too bright
the chain's too tight
the beast won't go to sleep
I've been running through
these promises to you
that I made and I could not keep

But a man never got a woman back
not by begging on his knees
or I'd crawl to you baby
and I'd fall at your feet
and I'd howl at your beauty
like a dog in heat
and I'd claw at your heart
and I'd tear at your sheet
I'd say please
    I'm your man

If you want got to sleep a moment on the road
I will steer for you
and if you want to work the street alone
I'll disappear for you
If you want a father
for your child
or only want to walk
with me a while
across the sand
    I'm your man

I CAN'T FORGET

I stumbled out of bed.
I got ready for the struggle.
I smoked a cigarette,
and I tightened up my gut.
I said, This can't be me,
must be my double.
And I can't forget
I can't forget
I can't forget
but I don't remember what.

I'm burning up the road.
I'm heading down to Phoenix.
I got this old address
of someone that I knew.
It was high and fine and free;
ah, you should have seen us!
And I can't forget
I can't forget
I can't forget
but I don't remember who.

I'll be there today
with a big bouquet
of cactus;
I got this rig that runs on memory.
And I promise,
cross my heart,
they'll never catch us,
but if they do
just say it was me.

I loved you all my life,
and that's how I want to end it.
The summer's almost gone.
The winter's tuning up.
Yeah, the summer's gone
but a lot goes on forever.
And I can't forget
I can't forget
I can't forget
but I can't remember what.

EVERYBODY KNOWS

Everybody knows that the dice are loaded. Everybody rolls with their fingers crossed. Everybody knows the war is over. Everybody knows the good guys lost. Everybody knows the fight was fixed: the poor stay poor, the rich get rich. That's how it goes. Everybody knows.

Everybody knows that the boat is leaking. Everybody knows the captain lied. Everybody got this broken feeling like their father or their dog just died. Everybody talking to their pockets. Everybody wants a box of chocolates and a long-stem rose. Everybody knows.

Everybody knows that you love me, baby. Everybody knows that you really do. Everybody knows that you've been faithful, give or take a night or two. Everybody knows you've been discreet but there were so many people you just had to meet without your clothes. And everybody knows.

Everybody knows that it's now or never. Everybody knows that it's me or you. Everybody knows that you live forever when you've done a line or two. Everybody knows the deal is rotten: Old Black Joe's still picking cotton for your ribbons and bows. Everybody knows.

Everybody knows that the Plague is coming. Everybody knows that it's moving fast. Everybody knows that the naked man and woman — just a shining artifact of the past. Everybody knows the scene is dead, but there's going to be a metre on your bed that will disclose what everybody knows.

Everybody knows that you're in trouble. Everybody knows what you've been through, from the bloody cross on top of Calvary to the beach at Malibu. Everybody knows it's coming apart: take one last look at this Sacred Heart before it blows. And everybody knows.

THE TOWER OF SONG

My friends are gone and my hair is grey.
I ache in the places where I used to play.
And I'm crazy for love but I'm not coming on.
I'm just paying my rent every day in the tower of song.

I said to Hank Williams, "How lonely does it get?"
Hank Williams hasn't answered yet,
but I hear him coughing all night long,
a hundred floors above me in the tower of song.

I was born like this, I had no choice.
I was born with the gift of a golden voice,
and twenty-seven angels from the great beyond,
they tied me to this table right here in the tower of song.

So you can stick your little pins in that voodoo doll
— I'm very sorry, baby, doesn't look like me at all.
I'm standing by the window where the light is strong.
They don't let a woman kill you, not in the tower of song.

Now you can say that I've grown bitter, but of this you may be sure:
The rich have got their channels in the bedrooms of the poor,
and there's a mighty judgement coming, but I may be wrong.
You see, you hear these funny voices in the tower of song.

I see you standing on the other side.
I don't know how the river got so wide.
I loved you, I loved you way back when —
And all the bridges are burning that we might have crossed,
but I feel so close to everything that we lost —
We'll never, we'll never have to lose it again.

So I bid you farewell, I don't know when I'll be back.
They're moving us tomorrow to that tower down the track.
But you'll be hearing from me, baby, long after I'm gone.
I'll be speaking to you sweetly from my window in the tower of song.

My friends are gone and my hair is grey.
I ache in the places where I used to play.
And I'm crazy for love, but I'm not coming on.
I'm just paying my rent every day in the tower of song.

THE FUTURE

DEMOCRACY

It's coming through a hole in the air,
from those nights in Tiananmen Square.
It's coming from the feel
that it ain't exactly real,
or it's real, but it ain't exactly there.
From the wars against disorder,
from the sirens night and day;
from the fires of the homeless,
from the ashes of the gay:
Democracy is coming to the U.S.A.

It's coming through a crack in the wall,
on a visionary flood of alcohol;
from the staggering account
of the Sermon on the Mount
which I don't pretend to understand at all.
It's coming from the silence
on the dock of the bay,
from the brave, the bold, the battered
heart of Chevrolet:
Democracy is coming to the U.S.A.

It's coming from the sorrow on the street,
the holy places where the races meet;
from the homicidal bitchin'
that goes down in every kitchen
to determine who will serve and who will eat.
From the wells of disappointment
where the women kneel to pray
for the grace of G-d in the desert here
and the desert far away:
Democracy is coming to the U.S.A.

Sail on, sail on
o mighty Ship of State!
To the Shores of Need
past the Reefs of Greed
through the Squalls of Hate
Sail on, sail on

It's coming to America first,
the cradle of the best and of the worst.
It's here they got the range
and the machinery for change
and it's here they got the spiritual thirst.
It's here the family's broken
and it's here the lonely say
that the heart has got to open
in a fundamental way:
Democracy is coming to the U.S.A.

It's coming from the women and the men.
O baby, we'll be making love again.
We'll be going down so deep
that the river's going to weep,
and the mountain's going to shout Amen!
It's coming like the tidal flood
beneath the lunar sway,
imperial, mysterious,
in amorous array:
Democracy is coming to the U.S.A.

Sail on, sail on
o mighty Ship of State!
To the Shores of Need
past the Reefs of Greed
through the Squalls of Hate
Sail on, sail on

I'm sentimental, if you know what I mean:
I love the country but I can't stand the scene.
And I'm neither left or right
I'm just staying home tonight,
getting lost in that hopeless little screen.
But I'm stubborn as those garbage bags
that Time cannot decay,
I'm junk but I'm still holding up
this little wild bouquet:
Democracy is coming to the U.S.A.

THE FUTURE

Give me back my broken night
my mirrored room, my secret life
It's lonely here,
there's no one left to torture
Give me absolute control
over every living soul
And lie beside me, baby,
that's an order!

Give me crack and anal sex
Take the only tree that's left
and stuff it up the hole
in your culture
Give me back the Berlin Wall
give me Stalin and St. Paul
I've seen the future, brother:
it is murder.

Things are going to slide in all directions
Won't be nothing
Nothing you can measure any more
The blizzard of the world
has crossed the threshold
and it has overturned
the order of the soul
When they said REPENT
I wonder what they meant

You don't know me from the wind
you never will, you never did
I'm the little jew
who wrote the bible
I've seen the nations rise and fall
I've heard their stories, heard them all
but love's the only engine of survival

Your servant here, he has been told
to say it clear, to say it cold:
It's over, it ain't going
any further
And now the wheels of heaven stop
you feel the devil's riding crop
Get ready for the future:
it is murder.

Things are going to slide in all directions

There'll be the breaking
of the ancient western code
Your private life will suddenly explode
There'll be phantoms
there'll be fires on the road
and the white man dancing
You'll see your woman
hanging upside down
her features covered by her fallen gown
and all the lousy little poets
coming round
trying to sound like Charlie Manson

Give me back the Berlin Wall
give me Stalin and St. Paul
Give me Christ
or give me Hiroshima
Destroy another fetus now
We don't like children anyhow
I've seen the future, baby:
it is murder.

Things are going to slide in all directions
Won't be nothing
Nothing you can measure any more
The blizzard of the world
has crossed the threshold
and it has overturned
the order of the soul
When they said REPENT
I wonder what they meant

ANTHEM

The birds they sang
at the break of day
Start again,
I heard them say,
Don't dwell on what
has passed away
or what is yet to be.

The wars they will
be fought again
The holy dove
be caught again
bought and sold
and bought again;
the dove is never free.

Ring the bells that still can ring.
Forget your perfect offering.
There is a crack in everything.
That's how the light gets in.

We asked for signs
the signs were sent:
the birth betrayed,
the marriage spent;
the widowhood
of every government —
signs for all to see.

Can't run no more
with that lawless crowd
while the killers in high places
say their prayers out loud.
But they've summoned up
a thundercloud
They're going to hear from me.

Ring the bells that still can ring
Forget your perfect offering.
There is a crack in everything.
That's how the light gets in.

You can add up the parts
but you won't have the sum
You can strike up the march,
there is no drum.
Every heart
to love will come
but like a refugee.

Ring the bells that still can ring
Forget your perfect offering.
There is a crack in everything.
That's how the light gets in.

LIGHT AS THE BREEZE

She stands before you naked
you can see it, you can taste it
but she comes to you
light as the breeze
You can drink or you can nurse it
it don't matter how you worship
as long as you're
down on your knees

So I knelt there at the delta
at the alpha and the omega
at the cradle of the river
and the seas
And like a blessing come from heaven,
for something like a second,
I was healed, and my heart
was at ease

O baby I waited
so long for your kiss
for something to happen
oh — something like this

And you're weak and you're harmless
and you're sleeping in your harness
and the wind going wild
in the trees
And it's not exactly prison
but you'll never be forgiven
for whatever you've done
with the keys

O baby I waited
so long for your kiss
for something to happen
oh — something like this

It's dark and it's snowing
I've got to be going
St. Lawrence River
is starting to freeze
And I'm sick of pretending
I'm broken from bending
I've lived too long
on my knees

And she dances so graceful
and your heart's hard and hateful
and she's naked
but that's just a tease
And you turn in disgust
from your hatred and from your love
and she comes to you
light as the breeze

O baby I waited
so long for your kiss
for something to happen
oh — something like this

There's blood on every bracelet
you can see it, you can taste it
and it's Please baby
please baby please
And she says, Drink deeply, pilgrim
but don't forget there's still a woman
beneath this
resplendent chemise

So I knelt there at the delta
at the alpha and the omega
I knelt there
like one who believes
And like a blessing come from heaven
for something like a second
I was cured, and my heart
was at ease

CLOSING TIME

So we're drinking and we're dancing
and the band is really happening
and the Johnny Walker wisdom running high
And my very sweet companion
she's the Angel of Compassion
and she's rubbing half the world against her thigh
Every drinker, every dancer
lifts a happy face to thank her
and the fiddler fiddles something so sublime
All the women tear their blouses off
and the men they dance on the polka-dots
and it's partner found and it's partner lost
and it's hell to pay when the fiddler stops
It's closing time

We're lonely, we're romantic
and the cider's laced with acid
and the Holy Spirit's crying, "Where's the beef?"
And the moon is swimming naked
and the summer night is fragrant
with a mighty expectation of relief
So we struggle and we stagger
down the snakes and up the ladder
to the tower where the blessed hours chime
And I swear it happened just like this:
a sigh, a cry, a hungry kiss
the Gates of Love they budged an inch
I can't say much has happened since
but closing time

I loved you for your beauty
but that doesn't make a fool of me —
you were in it for your beauty too
I loved you for your body
there's a voice that sounds like G-d to me
declaring that your body's really you
I loved you when our love was blessed
and I love you now there's nothing left
but sorrow and a sense of overtime
And I miss you since our place got wrecked
I just don't care what happens next
looks like freedom but it feels like death
it's something in between, I guess
it's closing time
And I miss you since the place got wrecked
by the winds of change and the weeds of sex
looks like freedom but it feels like death
it's something in between, I guess
it's closing time

We're drinking and we're dancing
but there's nothing really happening
the place is dead as Heaven on a Saturday night
And my very close companion
gets me fumbling, gets me laughing
she's a hundred but she's wearing something tight
And I lift my glass to the Awful Truth
which you can't reveal to the Ears of Youth
except to say it isn't worth a dime
And the whole damn place goes crazy twice
and it's once for the Devil and it's once for Christ
but the Boss don't like these dizzy heights —
we're busted in the blinding lights
of closing time

WAITING FOR THE MIRACLE

Baby, I've been waiting,
I've been waiting night and day.
I didn't see the time,
I waited half my life away.
There were lots of invitations
and I know you sent me some
but I was waiting
for the miracle to come.

I know you really loved me
but, you see, my hands were tied.
I know it must have hurt you,
it must have hurt your pride
to stand beneath my window
with your bugle and your drum
while I was waiting
for the miracle to come.

So you wouldn't like it, baby.
You wouldn't like it here.
There's not much entertainment
and the judgements are severe.
The maestro says it's Mozart
but it sounds like bubblegum
when you're waiting
for the miracle to come.

Waiting for the miracle
there's nothing left to do.
I haven't been this happy
since the end of World War II.
Nothing left to do
when you know that you've been taken.
Nothing left to do
when you're begging for a crumb.
Nothing left to do
when you've got to go on waiting,
waiting for the miracle to come.

I dreamed about you, baby.
It was just the other night.
Most of you was naked
but some of you was light.
The sands of time were falling
from your fingers and your thumb
and you were waiting
for the miracle to come.

Baby, let's get married,
we've been alone too long.
Let's be alone together,
let's see if we're that strong.
Let's do something crazy,
something absolutely wrong
while we're waiting
for the miracle to come.

Nothing left to do
when you know that you've been taken.
Nothing left to do
when you're begging for a crumb.
Nothing left to do
when you've got to go on waiting,
waiting for the miracle to come.

When you've fallen on the highway
and you're lying in the rain,
and they ask you how you're doing,
of course you say you can't complain —
if you're squeezed for information,
that's when you've got to play it dumb:
You just say you're out there waiting
for the miracle to come.

UNCOLLECTED POEMS

TO A FELLOW STUDENT

I thought about you a lot.
I still do.
You sat still,
your hands clasped on your lap
like a schoolchild.
You were allowed to cry
because you have been true
to your grief.
I saw you today
sitting in the same way,
the same tears on your cheeks,
as if you had not moved
in all these years —
the same bad headache
in your right eye,
the same housefly
trying to fertilize your lips.
Old friend, you're a mess
by every measure
except the ladder of love.

Jemez Springs, 1980

FRAGMENT FROM A JOURNAL

I lit a stick of incense. I sat down on a small cushion crossing my legs in a full Lotus. For over an hour I thought about how much I hated one of my ex-wives.

It was still dark when I began writing a metaphysical song called "Letter to the Christians," in which I attempted to exaggerate the maturity of my own religious experience and invalidate everyone else's, especially those who claimed a renewed spiritual vitality.

Several days later I had four stanzas of eight lines each, which certified that I received the Holy Spirit, attained to a deep enlightenment, circumcised my soul with the Wine of Love, and "accustomed myself to the clemency of the Lord."

I told the song to Anthony that afternoon as we were standing knee deep in the Aegean Sea. We had a good laugh. He especially liked this verse:

> The imitations of His love
> He sponsors patiently
> Until you can be born with Him
> some hopeless night in Galilee
> until you lose your pride in Him
> until your faith objective fails
> until you stretch your arms so wide
> you do not need these Roman nails

A few minutes later Anthony produced a reply:

> I really hope you stumble on
> The Great Red Whore of Babylon
> Forget the Grace
> Enjoy the Lace
> Have some fun and carry on

He is very fast. The beach was full of beautiful young women whom I desired uniformly at a very low intensity. I saw a new-born Christian on a rock contemplating the beauty of His Handiwork and I hurried off to let her know that I had been touched by Grace. My song almost made her cry. She hadn't known "that I knew the Lord."

Hydra, 1983

WHEN EVEN THE

Your breasts are like.
Your thighs and your carriage.
I never thought.
Somewhere there must be.
It's possible.
Summer has nothing.
Even Spring doesn't.
Your feet are so.
It's cruel to.
My defence is.
Summer certainly doesn't.
Your.
And your.
If only.
Somewhere there must.

But the.
And the.
It's enough to.
Soldiers don't.
Prisoners don't.
Maybe the turtle.
Maybe hieroglyphics.
Sand.
But in your cold.
If I could.
If once more.
Slip or liquid.
But the.
And the.

Sometimes when.
Even tho'.
Yes even tho'.
They say suffering.
They say.
Okay then let's.
Let's.
The sign is.
The seal is.
The guarantee.
Oh but.
O cruel.
O blouse with.
This is what.
And why it isn't.

But what do they.
What do they.
When even.
When even the.
Years will.
Death will.
But they won't.
Even if.
Even if the.
They never will.

O deceiver.
O deceptive.
Turn your eyes.
Incline your.
To the one who.
Rotten as.
Who does not.
Who never will.

But now your.
And your.
And these arms.
Which is lawless.
Which is blind.
If you come.
If you find.
Then I.

Like all.
Like every.
If only.
If when.
Even though.
Even if.
Not for.
Not for.
But only.
But every.

If I could.
When the.
Then I.
Even if.
Even when.
I would.

New York, 1982

PARIS MODELS

The models were changing
for the next shot.
I saw the sex of one
and the breast of another.
A balloon was taped
to a woman's finger,
and they started up
the wind machine.
The dresses came alive
and glorious accidents
of hair and shadow
framed their solemn faces.
The miracle of the balloon
grazing on a fingertip,
while the storm
carried off their bodies,
was deeply convincing.
Finally the Chinese food arrived,
and the models walked around
wearing towels
and carrying paper plates.
Everyone was happy
that the magic of womanhood
had worked again.
They could rest a little while
on the great wave,
at the very crest

of confident and effortless allure.
I was happy too.
I felt privileged
to have attended a ceremony
usually restricted to professionals.

Paris, 1987

ON SEEING KABIR'S POEMS
ON HER DRESSING TABLE

Perfumed soap
    and a little Kabir
another hundred thousand
    and a little Kabir
A new stone house, a swimming pool
arguments, debts, and facials, facials
    and here is Kabir's Love Swing
    here is his Apartment of Death
Kabir, you old braggart
you have put them all to sleep

Rousillon, 1981

MY HONOUR

My honour is in bad shape.
I'm crawling at a woman's feet.
She doesn't give an inch.
I look good for fifty-two
but fifty-two is fifty-two.
I'm not even a Zen Master.
I'm this man in a blue summer suit.
My lawyer took my .32 away
and locked it in the safe.
I'm defenceless against
her arrogance.
When the world is slow
she turns to me for an easy victory.
I'll rise up one of these days,
find my way to the airport.
I'll rise up and say
I loved you better than you loved me
and then I'll die for a long time
at the centre of my own dismal organization,
and I'll remember today,
the day when I was that asshole in a blue summer suit
who couldn't take it any longer.

Paris, 1987

PEACE

I've come clean
I'm afraid you will have to bow down to me
I won't be able to breathe properly
unless I am worshipped
You thought I was getting better
didn't you
Here it comes again
peace
the hands of peace around my throat
That's why I'm letting you go
that's why I'm sitting here
in my robes
with my eyes rolled back into my head

Mt. Baldy, 1980

THE EMBRACE

When you stumble suddenly
into his full embrace,
he hides away so not to see
his creature face to face.
You yourself are hidden too,
with all your sins of state;
there is no king to pardon you;
his mercy is more intimate.

He does not stand before you,
he does not dwell within;
this passion has no point of view,
it is the heart of everything.
There is no hill to see this from.
You share one body now
with the serpent you forbid,
and with the dove that you allow.

The imitations of his love
he suffers patiently,
until you can be born with him
some hopeless night in Galilee;
until you lose your pride in him,
until your faith objective fails,
until you stretch your arms so wide
you do not need these Roman nails.

Idolators on every side,
they make an object of the Lord.
They hang him on a cross so high

that you must ever move toward.
They bid you cast the world aside
and hurl your prayers at him.
Then the idol-makers dance all night
upon your suffering.

But when you rise from his embrace
I trust you will be strong and free
and tell no tales about his face,
and praise Creation joyously.

Hydra, 1983

A DEEP HAPPINESS

A deep happiness
    has seized me
My Christian friends say
that I have received
    the Holy Spirit
It is only the truth of solitude
It is only the torn anemone
fastened to the rock
    its root exposed
to the off-shore wind
O friend of my scribbled life
your heart is like mine —
your loneliness
    will bring you home

Hydra, 1981

EVERY PEBBLE

Every pebble dreams of itself
Every leaf has a scheme
The sun is by desire bound
to travel down a beam
Defeated still I cannot yield
my heart to blessed peace
because I dream that there are chains
I dream there is release

I told this to the prisoner
who killed the man I hate
I told it to the miner who
dug up my golden plate
Therefore do I live in hell
for dreaming that hell is
the distance that I dare to put
between my hand and his

I dreamed my body yesternight
I dreamed the universe
I dreamed I dreamed a thousand years
in order to rehearse
the seven days of wonderment
when, drawn from the mist
I was clothed in nakedness
and suffered to exist

I dreamed that I was given song
to be my only proof
that my true dwelling place with you
has neither ground nor roof

nor windows to look out of, Lord
nor mirrors to look in
nor singing to be out of it
nor dying to begin

O child this is your human dream
this is your human sleep
and do not strive so hard to climb
from what is sound and deep
I love the dream that you've begun
beneath my evergreen
I love the pebble and the sun
and all that's in between

And for this conversation
in the early morning light
I offer up these shabby days
that fray before your sight
Nor can I know how many more
will pass ere I'm unstrung
and all that's left this song you placed
upon your creature's tongue

Montreal, 1978

400

DAYS OF KINDNESS

Greece is a good place
to look at the moon, isn't it
You can read by moonlight
You can read on the terrace
You can see a face
as you saw it when you were young
There was good light then
oil lamps and candles
and those little flames
that floated on a cork in olive oil
What I loved in my old life
I haven't forgotten
It lives in my spine
Marianne and the child
The days of kindness
It rises in my spine
and it manifests as tears
I pray that a loving memory
exists for them too
the precious ones I overthrew
for an education in the world

Hydra, 1985

INDEX OF TITLES

INDEX OF FIRST LINES

410

412